# SUCCESSFUL SIGN DESIGN

# SUCCESSFUL SIGN DESIGN

By the editors of **Signs of the Times** magazine

Retail Reporting Corporation, New York

Retail Reporting Corporation
101 Fifth Avenue
New York, NY 10003

Distributors to the trade in the United States and Canada:
Van Nostrand Reinhold
115 Fifth Avenue
New York, NY 10003

Distributed outside of the United States and Canada:
Hearst Books International
105 Madison Avenue
New York, NY 10016

Library of Congress Cataloging in Publication Data:
Main Entry under the title: Successful Sign Design

Printed and Bound in Hong Kong
ISBN 0-934590-28-1

Designed by Judy Shepard

1154552

# CONTENTS

# INTRODUCTION

Few factors permeate modern day living as pervasively as the sign. Yet, as apparent as sign identification is, it continuously runs the risk of being overlooked. Historically, sign identification traces its roots to mankind's earliest communication, as evidenced by the earliest cave drawings. In recent years, however, sign design has been considered equal in importance to the sign message. The philosophy behind the design has undergone more changes in the last ten years than in any previous period. It is no longer considered effective or acceptable for the sign's design to be less important than its informational content.

Design trends today appear to be going in two notable

directions: One distinctive outlet is taking sign design to a clean look where identification by faster moving traffic is required. The other outlet is to an ornate, crafted appearance primarily intended to recapture the nostalgic seal of times when the world moved more slowly.

The modern-day sign industry is equipped with the tools, materials, skills and technology to fulfill even the most challenging identity project. Its product range runs the gamut from steel, stainless steel, aluminum, plastics, woods, concrete, glass, gold leaf, paints, and more, available in a multiplicity of colors, textures and patterns. From the illumination standpoint, the palette includes direct, indirect, and silhouette lightings by fluorescent and incandescent lamps, floods, metal hailides, luminous tubings and even lasers and fiber optics. Successful Sign Design demonstrates the skill and ability of the industry in over 300 photographs culled from submissions to the annual design contest sponsored by the sign industry' journal Signs of the Times. The intention, however, is not only to showcase the industry's most outstanding work to date, but to offer a review of the gamut of contemporary sign design, from the industry mainstays — i.e. ground, interior and wall-mounted signage — to the specialities — i.e. glass and window signs — to the fairly new developments — i.e. illuminated awnings — entering the sign design vernacular.

# GROUND SIGNS

GROUND SIGNS, including both the low profile type as well as the pylon or post-mounted variety, are a sign industry mainstay, suitable for identifying and advertising every type of business and/or service. Ground signs may be illuminated or non-illuminated; wood or metal; handlettered or spray painted — every method and material is conducive to this variety of signage. Although physically independent of the building it identifies, the ground sign should relate to the building's design as well as its surroundings.

Designer: Merv Eckman
Fabricator: Adcon Signs
Ft. Collins, CO
Client: Market Square Shopping Center

Interior illuminated sign fabricated from the ''ABC''
bleed palls extrusion system with sign-o-flex faces.

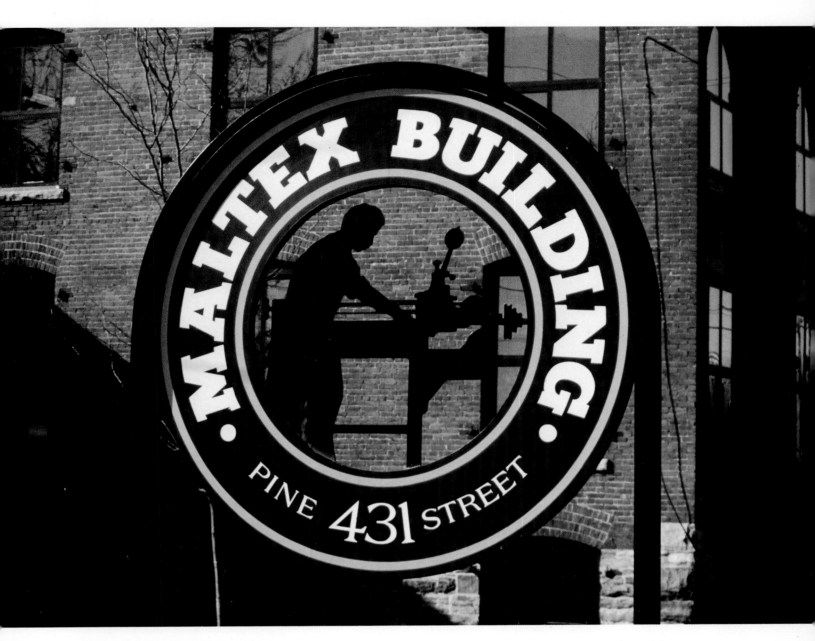

Designer:    Sparky Potter
Fabricator:   Wood & Wood
               Waitsfield, VT
Client:       The Davis Company

Channelled-metal post structure and 1/8'' metal
sandwiched into two layers of MDO.

Designer:    Andre Probst Creative Design Inc.
Fabricator:   Andre Probst Creative Design Inc.
               Kitchener, Ontario, Canada
Client:       Ginty Jocius & Associates

Triangular ground sign is fabricated of polycarbonate
laminated to MDO, finished on the first surface with a
matte silver. Changeable tenant panel is illuminated with
fluorescent V-lamps. Overall height: 6'4''.

13

Designer: Barry S. Rawson
Fabricator: B B Signs
Lake Geneva, WI
Client: A Day In The Country

4'x8' M.D.O. cut-out sign is mounted on slotted 4''x6'' posts.

Designer: Lee-Rovtar Associates
Fabricator: SmithCraft Mfg., Inc.
Phoenix, AZ
Client: Hyatt-Gainey Ranch

Patina-finish copper sign panel is cut-out; copy is polished brass.

Designer: Lori Logan
Fabricator: Amidon & Co., Inc.
Sandwich, MA
Client: The Crystal Pineapple

24''x30'' sign is fabricated from 8/4 lumber.
Handcarved raised numbers and letters are gilded. Solid crystal pineapple was customer provided. The pineapple is bracketed with a lockable arm that is embedded into the sign.

Designer:      Woodmark
Fabricator:    Woodmark - Harry Wheeler,
               Bernard Jones
               Akron, OH
Client:        The Branigar Organization, Inc.

18'x5'6½'' (7' overall height) x 11¼'' thick solid,
douglas fir timber pressure treated with clear
preservative, thru bolted. Hand carved graphics.
Finished with oil stain and gold leaf.

Designer:     Delainie Cornwall and Sparky Potter
Fabricator:   Wood & Wood Design Company
              Waitsfield, VT
Client:       The Treasure Ship

Basswood lamination woodburned and painted
illustration, 7 coats of varnish finish; approx. 5'x2½'.

Designer:      Jim Elbers
Fabricator:    Don Bell & Co.
               Port Orange, FL
Client:        Trailinn

Double face internally illuminated sign moulded acrylic
faces with embossed logo and main copy. Center panel
in pylon cover illuminates. Aluminum pylon cover with
stucco finish.

Designer:     F.R.E.A. - Jim Staples
Fabricator:   Front Range Electrical Advertising, Inc.
              Denver, CO
Client:       Lincor Properties of Colorado

The (3) sided illuminated display. Sheetmetal skirting
top and bottom. 1/8'' routed out aluminum faces
backed with white plex. The display incorporates
indirect lighting above and below the sign faces,
creating a halo effect around the peach skirtings.

Designer:     Ronald E. Pomerleau
Fabricator:   Roland's Neon Sign Co. Ltd.
              Windsor, Ontario, Canada
Client:       Hilton

2'x2'x10' four-sided direction display uses white acrylic
faces with exterior graphics. Base uses ceramic tile
borrowing from hotel lobby.

Designer: Bryan Scott/Venton Shrewsbury
Fabricator: Innovations Signs & Designs
Client: Star Builders Inc.

A single-faced sandblasted redwood sign measuring
2'x6' for an exclusive, secluded housing development.
This project required capturing the natural surroundings
and habitat. The lake scenery and largemouth bass
were painted with a combination of brush and airbrush
techniques. The grid pattern, surrounding the lake was
accomplished with rabbit wire applied, then blasted.
The post panels are of cedar that were rounded at the
top and then blasted to create a rough mountain
backdrop.

Designer: Richard Molacek
Fabricator: Weathertop Woodcraft and Sign
Wheaton, IL
Client: Glencrest of Inverness

Finished size: 8'x6' (at top of sign), 12''x12'' posts.
Sign and posts made of western red cedar, background
small lettering — sandblasted — geese of sugarpine
applied and carved. Top cap bent from ¼'' stock (built
up lamination).

Designer: John T. Delich-Executive Hills, Inc.
Fabricator: Star Signs & Graphics, Inc. ·
Overland Park, KS
Client: Executive Hills Inc.

Fabricated aluminum construction with routed graphics.
Stainless steel logo with #8 polished finish. Internally
illuminated with flourescent.

Designer: Andre Probst
Fabricator: Andre Probst Creative Design Inc.
Kitchener, Ontario, Canada
Client: Versa-Care Limited &
Cambridge Memorial Hospital

Sheet metal construction finished in polyurethane
enamel, 4'x 10' flush mounted polycarbonate faces.
Finished in opaque white on first surface. Texture:
Sprayed concrete base with aluminum individual
numbers. Graphics are dark blue and grey (Versa-Care
logo) when non-illuminated. (Both photos show
illumination.) Overall height 11'8''.

Designer: Wondriska Associates
Fabricator: Sign-Lite Inc.
North Hanover, CT
Client: The Phoenix Insurance Co.

4'x 4' cube — 14' high, 1/4'' aluminum plate; 1/4''
polished brass letters. Stencil cut, back-lit logos cut
from 1/8'' aluminum plate.

Designer: Waggoner-Shumate
Fabricator: Sign Artists
Rogers, AK
Client: Waggoner-Shumate

Sign is painted on MDO plywood. Frame is 2'' angle iron from original sign, which was changed to run vertically rather than horizontally. Background is black with white letters and rainbow logo. Final coating of sign finish clear gave clean, dramatic effect.

Fabricator: Gordon Sign Company
Denver, CO
Client: Denver Seminary

This double-faced display is 5'x18' which features an aluminum face with routed copy and graphics. The faces project from a common base and the bottom of the cabinet returns to the base at a 45° angle. It is internally illuminated with T-12 lamps.

Designer: Thomas Brown/Valley City Sign Co.
Fabricator: Valley City Sign Company
Comstock Park, MI
Client: Dickenson Press

Double-faced, internally illuminated, low profile sign with bleed off flexible sign face.

Designer: Jim deRoin and Todd Kershner
Fabricator: Todd Kershner
Denver, CO
Client: Bill Benson & Assoc.

The pictorial portion of this single-sided redwood sign was sandblasted to several different depths, carved, airbrushed and handpainted. The ornate lower part of the sign was routed and handcarved with a dark-colored stain airbrushed into recesses to heighten the detail. Both 23K and red varnished goldleaf were applied to the ''Historic Area'' copy. The sign measures 30'' x 36''.

Designer:    Jimmy Poe
Fabricator:  Sun Graphics, Inc.
             Myrtle Beach, NC
Client:      Southcreek

The 2 signs form entrance walls on either side of the
road. The signs are 2'' sandblasted redwood, using
multiple layers on the logo. The faces are attached to
masonary walls which have been stucco covered and
painted. Approximately 5'x14'.

Designer: Foster Conant & Assoc.
Fabricator: Envirographics, Inc.
Client: The Parkway

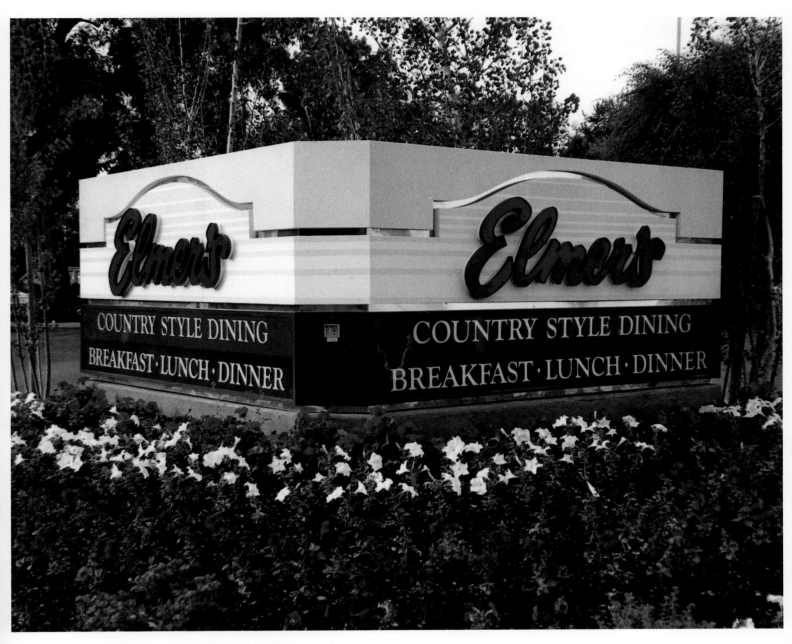

Designer:    Mack Bachman, Byron Knight
Fabricator:   Image National
              Boise, IA
Client:      Elmers Country Style Dining

Designer:      Harlan Miller/Harlan Adv.
Fabricator:    Simon Sign Co.
               Cleveland, OH
Client:        The Front Row

Designer:      Peter McGoldrick
Fabricator:    Oregon Sign Corporation
               Portland, OR
Client:        Meadow Creek

Acrylic background. Internally illuminated with
fluorescents. Sheet metal pylon painted with texcote
finish. Sign is installed in brick planter over small
pool and fountain.

Designer: Jim Bolek
Fabricator: The Signs & Service Co.
Phoenix, AZ
Client: Desert Palm Plaza

The sign incorporates 6'x12' ceramic tile with
sandblasted copy. It includes a steel cabinet with solid
copper borders and logo. White neon provides the
backlit illumination. The base is stucco.

MAY
18
~
22

WHITAKER

COMPETITION

Designer: Bill Christman
Fabricator: Christman Studios
St. Louis, MO
Client: CASA (Community Action School
of the Arts)

5' x 15' plywood sign is handlettered to promote an international piano competition. The intention was to design a bold colored sculptural collage, using the existing, drab pylon sign as the base.

Designer: Full Moon Signs & Graphics
Fabricator: Full Moon Signs & Graphics
Tallahassee, FL
Client: Investors Real Estate Management, Inc.

4'x6' double-faced painted panels are encased in a 2'' x 6'' framework, supported on 6''x6'' posts.

Designer: Full Moon Signs & Graphics
Fabricator: Full Moon Signs & Graphics
Tallahassee, FL
Client: Investors Real Estate Management, Inc.

4' x 4' D/F double-faced sign is framed with 2'' x 6'' cedar. Colors coordinate w/buildings. ''Cherry branch'' edge is used on secondary directional and parking signage.

| | | |
|---|---|---|
| Designer: | Sign Consultants, Inc. | Internally illuminated free standing sign; aluminum skin |
| Fabricator: | Cragg Sign | over aluminum angle frame; transluscent flexible faces |
| | Golden Valley, MN | with heat transfer graphics. |
| Client: | Kraus Anderson Realty/ | |
| | Valley Ridge Shopping Center | |

Designer:      Envirographics, Inc.
Fabricator:    Envirographics, Inc.
               Orlando, FL
Client:        Condev

15' high ''v'' shaped monument sign constructed in
block with stucco finish and granite cladding. Logo is
cut out 1/4'' aluminum with anodized clear finish.
Letters are 3/8'' aluminum.

Designer: Bill Chappell/ADCON Signs
Fabricator: ADCON Signs
     Fort Collins, CO
Client: Stanley Village

Interiorly illuminated flexible face sign effects a natural look with wood timbers and native moss rock.

Designer: Bentsen Signs
Fabricator: Bentsen Signs
     East Greenwich, RI
Client: Antique-Boutique

The 5'x7' main sign consists of a carved center panel (with 23K gold letters) which floats between two redwood panels for subcopy (dark browns). The 3-D beveled look is achieved with eight redwood moldings which picture frame the sign's face and eight copper-colored cap moldings (anodized aluminum) which box the sign in.

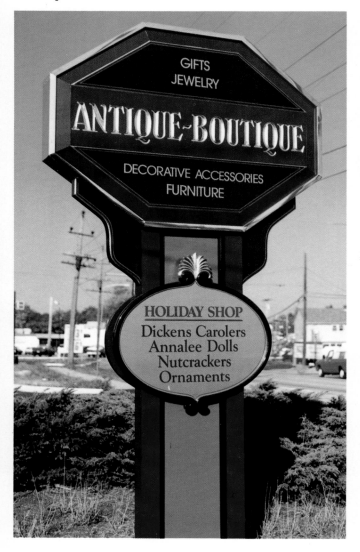

Designer: Craig Neon, Inc.
Fabricator: Craig Neon, Inc.
     Tulsa, OK
Client: Tulsa Design Center

Anchor tenants flexible face sign combined with conventional acrylic signs for other tenants. Stucco pole covers, neon accents and hot-transfer vinyl graphics complete system.

Designer:     Layco Sign Company
Fabricator:    American Sign and Indicator Corp.
                 Spokane, WA
Client:        Tobies Mill

Sandblasted wood pictorial on wood pylon with
illuminated plastic faced copy. Message center features
computer-controlled animation.

Designer: The CGF Design Group
Fabricator: Gordon Sign Company
Denver, CO
Client: The Writer Corporation

The designers used the detailing from the building and integrated the sign structure into the existing site walls. The sign forms a pavilion over the pedestrian entrance to the complex. The sign pushes the limits of electronic display technology with three single faces displaying the same message. Each face is 72 bulbs across and 24 bulbs deep allowing the user up to 3 lines of 15'' copy and/or graphics and animation across all three sign faces. All three faces are driven from a single remote terminal.

Designer: Richard Lang
Fabricator: Lawrence Signs, Inc.
St. Paul, MN
Client: Brookview Plaza

The exposed neon is mounted on an aluminum cabinet.
The ''Brookview Plaza'' letters have been routed with
1'' clear acrylic pushed through, then internally
illuminated.

Designer:      Andre Probst Creative Design Inc.
Fabricator:    Andre Probst Creative Design Inc.
               Kitchener, Ontario, Canada
Client:        Kitchener-Waterloo Hospital

Sheet metal construction finished in polyurethane enamel, flush mounted polycarbonate faces, finished on first surface in opaque off-white. Sign face is 4'x10'; overall height is 16'.

Designer:      K.C. Conrad/United Sign Corp.
Fabricator:    United Sign Corporation
               Green Bay, WI
Client:        Sunrise Savings

Four-sided sign is illuminated with four mercury vapor lamps, polycarbonate face, two single-face time and temp. units in an aluminum structure. Corrugation is formed from .040 aluminum sheets. Facials are fastened from the inside of the cube.

Designer:      Claude Neon
Fabricator:    Claude Neon
               Winnipeg, Manitoba, Canada
Client:        NormanView Mall

Pylon sign is 8' deep x 10'6'' wide x 30' high, and illuminated with mercury vapor lamps.

Designer:    Alan Welner Designs
Fabricator:  Signed Statement, Inc.
             Phoenix, AZ
Client:      The Plaza Tower

This major ID sign is 17' high and 7' wide with an arched top following the forms found in the midrise tower. It is internally illuminated with routed faces of .125'' aluminum. Letters and logo are infilled with opaque acrylic with a 1/4'' outline of transluscent white acrylic producing a halo appearance when illuminated. A 2'' polished copper reveal separates a painted concrete base from the copy panels. Four removable tenant copy panels have standardized type color, size and style.

Designer:      Alan Welner Designs
Fabricator:    Smithcraft Mfg. Inc.
               Phoenix, AZ
Client:        The Symington Company

This 25' high project development sign is composed of a 6'' diameter steel tube armature in the form of the project logo. Exposed white neon is attached to the ''spokes'' as well as within the 18'' open channel letters. The main copy panel is fabricated from aluminum. A serpentine screen wall is fabricated from M.D.O. and flat cut out project logos. Landscaping has been integrated to highlight the sign which has become a landmark at one of the busiest intersections in Phoenix.

Designer:      Barlo Signs
Fabricator:    Barlo Signs
               Hudson, NH
Client:        Nashoba Valley Banking Center

Pylon, 11'x 8''x 10' overall. Double-faced, internally illuminated fluorescent 4''x 4'' steel frame. 3'x 10' sign.

Designer:     The Ramos Group
Fabricator:   Star Signs & Graphics, Inc.
              Overland Park, KS
Client:       Oak Park Commons

This sign has a fabricated aluminum construction with
routed graphics and projecting clear acrylic letters. It is
both internally illuminated and floodlit externally. The
brick construction matches the buildings in the
shopping center.

Designer:     Alan Welner Designs
Fabricator:   Bleier Industries
              Phoenix, AZ
Client:       Country Club Manor

The logo cabinet within the sign is fabricated from
aluminum, polished brass and illuminated white acrylic
and is framed by brick, stucco and marble. Polished
brass, reverse pan channel address numbers are flush-
mounted to the brick sign structure.

Designer:     Gary Anderson
Fabricator:   Bloomington Design
              Bloomington, IN
Client:       The Country Gentlemen

Handlettered, airbrushed sign has marbled initials and
asphaltum shadows.

Designer:      Ireland, Peachey & Company
Fabricator:    Ireland, Peachey & Company
               North Vancouver, B.C., Canada
Client:        Westminster Quay Public Market

Free standing display to hold advertising posters. Made
from painted particle board, the sign reflects the post-
modernist design and color scheme of the market
building.

Designer:     Gene Costa
Fabricator:   Federal Sign
              Dublin, CA
Client:       Maestro's Caffe Italiano

The customer requested a contemporary logo for his
restaurant. The sign has a white acrylic background
with overlays of black and green vinyls.

Designer: Peterson/Griffin Architect, Ltd.
Fabricator: General Sign
West Newton, MA
Client: Prospect Hill Hotel Limited Partnership

Designer: Ronald E. Pomerleau
Fabricator: Roland's Neon Sign Co. Ltd.
          Windsor, Ontario, Canada
Client: Majestic Electronic Super Store

6'x24'6'' pylon uses acrylic faces with internally processed graphics. Aluminum frames and cabinets are finished yellow to match graphics.

Designer: Craig Neon, Inc.
Fabricator: Craig Neon, Inc.
          Tulsa, OK
Client: Manchester Square Shopping Center

Retainerless flexible sign faces with sculptured pole covers accented with neon.

Designer: Craig Neon, Inc.
Fabricator: Craig Neon, Inc.
Tulsa, OK
Client: Otasco

Curved aluminum structure, covered with stucco.
Individual illuminated letters mounted to structure.
Approximate size 6'x32'. Day and night photos shown.

Designer: Jones Sign Systems
Fabricator: Jones Sign Systems
Eugene, OR
Client: Riverpark Living Center

Routed aluminum backed up with white acrylic and
internally illuminated. The top cap is polished aluminum
and is removable for service access. The trim on
building was painted to match sign.

Designer: Z Studio
Fabricator: Andco Industries Corp.
Greensboro, NC
Client: Deborah Heart and Lung Center

Sign is manufactured from aluminum with cut-out
graphics backed with acrylic.

Designer: Christopher Boehm
Fabricator: Kieffer & Co., Inc.
Woodstock, GA
Client: Bank Atlanta

Routed gold mirrored stainless steel faces backed with
pre-fabricated aluminum cabinet and pole covers.

Designer:      Bill Thoman, Larry Catton
Fabricator:    Acme Neon Signs (Windsor) Ltd.
                Windsor, Ontario, Canada
Client:         Acme Neon Signs

This sign is a four-sided cube with faces consisting of
6'x6' retrofit, frameless heat-transfered flexible face
material, with two double-faced 18'' time and
temperature displays. The pylon and time-and-
temperature enclosure consist of a ⅛'' aluminum top
cube that rotates 90° every 10 minutes and remains
stationary except for the rotating time of approximately
five seconds.

| Designer: | J.R. Haller Ltd. |
| Fabricator: | J.R. Haller Ltd. |
| | Columbus, OH |
| Client: | Ruff Business Interiors |

This 20'-high triangular-shaped monolith is 5'x5'x4' with a 6'' polished stainless steel front edge stripe with original graphics cut out of .150 aluminum and backed up with white acrylic. The unit also has a time-and-temperature system. Paint finish is black suede catalyst.

Designer: Bob Dail & Ray Toraby
Fabricator: Craig Neon, Inc. (CNI)
Tulsa, OK
Client: Bridgeport Office Park

Retainerless flexible sign face with opaque blue background and grey graphics. Bottom section designed for major tenant (also internally illuminated).

Designer: Raul Garcia
Fabricator: Federal Sign
Houston, TX
Client: Valley Centre

Background is 1/8'' aluminum plate with routed-out copy illuminated by 800ma high output fluorescent lamps. Pole cover is clear anodized aluminum.

John R. Hunt, M.D., P.A.
Surgery & Endoscopy

Anderson
Oncology & Hemotology
Clinic, P.A.
Rajeev Malik, M.D.

703

Designer:    William Hopper
Fabricator:   City Sign Company
             Seneca, SC
Client:      John R. Hunt, M.D.

9'x 5½'x 4'' thick redwood. Sign has 4''x 4'' on end
that hinges down to remove blasted panels that slide out
on a track. Number is carved and gilded.

Designer:      Mary Head, Latham Brefka Assoc.
Fabricator:    Uxbridge Carvers
               Uxbridge, MA
Client:        Codex

Mahagony — carved S.F. 10'8'' x 18''. Gold leaf.

Designer:      William Tiley
Fabricator:    Gemini Sign & Design Ltd.
               Conway, NH
Client:        The Moats

18''x8' sandblasted redwood — original illustration
painted in lettering paint. This is an actual view of Moat
Mountain.

Designer:     Mark Jolley
Fabricator:   Young Electric Sign Co.
              West Sacramento, CA
Client:       Sherwood Corners

Aluminum composite board was used to sheet this 50'
double-faced monument sign. A six-line (48 x 72
matrix) electronic message center is recessed into the
faces. Eighteen-inch polished stainless steel, backlit
reverse pan channel letters are mounted above the
message center.

Designer:     Envirographics, Inc.
Fabricator:   Envirographics, Inc.
              Orlando, FL

Two of these 5'x25' pylon signs identify a 49-acre
business park. Four millimeter steel panels were rolled
in sections with graphics cut through later and backed
with acrylic. A steel substructure holds the panels in
place, and five 15mm bands of neo blue neon crown the
tops of the signs.

Designer: William Hopper
Fabricator: City Sign Company
Seneca, SC
Client: Baron Agency

Clear redwood construction. Deer handcarved finished in acrylic 3'x12'.

Designer:    Michael Steimle
Fabricator:  Comet Neon & Plastic Signs
             Escondido, CA
Client:      Woolley's Petite Suites

Materials. . . metal, plex, wood, neon, T-12. Illuminated
plex. letters and sheep. . . 2'' jewelite at edge of letters
and sheep with yellow edgelight. Red neon cove light
behind red border on texcoat opaque plex. Background
wood supports.

Designer:      Art & Sign of Toledo
Fabricator:    Art & Sign of Toledo
               Toledo, OH
Client:        Kensington Investors

.050 aluminum cabinet, cut-out acrylic letters and
exposed neon.

Designer:	Sign Language
Fabricator:	Sign Language
	Hopewell Junction, NY
Client:	B&B Auto Specialists

Entire sign structure is fabricated from .040 baked
enamel aluminum. Faces, letters, striping and graphics
fabricated from acrylic. Illumination via fluorescent tubes
from ground level up.

Fabricator:	Sign-O-Lite
	Richmond, B.C., Canada
Client:	Impact Plaza

Low profile four-sided rotating display — 6'x8'. Design
and color of display ties into the architecture of the
building.

Designer: Sparky Potter
Fabricator: Wood & Wood
Waitsfield, VT
Client: Steve Briggs

Using summer and winter scenes helps the awareness level of the public and keeps the boredom in painting away. Post system is hemlock and sign face is a combination of MDO for the letters and basswood for the painting.

Designer: Arteffects, Inc.
Fabricator: Arteffects, Inc.
Hartford, CT
Client: Margaritaville

5'x 6'x 5/8'' duraply panels on framework of 2x4's. Copy and illustration painted with enamels and artist's oils.

Designer: Steven L. Miller
Fabricator: SignWorks
Lantana, FL
Client: The Cutting Room

3/4'' MDO double-faced sign is mounted on 6'' x 6'' post and handpainted with a matte finish. Scissors are handcarved.

MARGARITAVILLE

**A Mexican Restaurant & Watering Hole**

Designer:      John R. Stenko
Fabricator:    Federal Sign
               Duluth, GA
Client:        Lanier Bank & Trust Company

The top section of this sign is .125 aluminum with wood moldings; the logo is routed with painted gold on yellow acrylic; the copy is routed with 1'' clear polished acrylic and black acrylic faces. It appears halo lighted at night. The sign is double-faced with a 15'' character time and temperature unit between the brick columns.

Designer:      Jimmy Poe
Fabricator:    Sun Graphics, Inc.
               Myrtle Beach, SC
Client:        Wachesaw Plantation

This 5'10'' x 13'' main indentification sign is fabricated of tongue-and groove cypress boards on the background, with multi-level wood molding on the top and bottom. The logo and secondary copy are constructed of ¼'' saw plate aluminum with offset stud mounting. The primary copy consists of polished ¼'' brass letters offset-mounted on ¾'' duraply cut-out letters.

Designer:     Thorough-Graphic Signs
Fabricator:    Thorough-Graphic Signs
                Lexington, KY
Client:       Hillenmeyer Nurseries

3' x 8' MDO faces boxed with aluminum frame. Cedar
posts are 6'' x 6'' with diagonal-cut rough-sawn tongue
and groove cedar. Flower cut-outs are airbrushed.

Designer: Jay Cooke/Tracy Dunphy/Ann Stafford
Fabricator: Jay Cooke's Sign Shop
Stowe, VT
Client: Amano

2'x6'' MDO sign is handlettered and airbrushed.
''Llama'' is flat gilded over sand smalt to provide
texture.

Designer:    Sign Consultants Inc.
Fabricator:   Lawrence Signs, Inc.
             St. Paul, MN
Client:       Midwest Auto Mall

Project identification and tenant listing with architectural feel. Constructed of building materials (block, stucco, metal roof) with two aluminum cans. Upper can with individual neon letters and exposed neon band and city location. Tenant panels routed and backed by plexiglas.

Designer:    Eric Morrell/Creel Morrell Inc.
Fabricator:   Adlite Signs, Inc.
             Austin, TX
Client:       Trammel Crow Company

A 28' brick pylon reminiscent of the architectural design of the retail center. ''The Colonade'' is 18'' high channel letters, open channel trapezoid on top is 15mm exposed red neon.

Designer: Richard C. Bowen & Assoc., Inc.
         Kieffer & Co.
Fabricator: Kieffer & Co., Inc.
         Park City, IL
Client: Melvin Simon & Associates

The two low profile signs fabricated using aluminum with a light grey textured finish matching the buildings in the retail center. The fabricated frontlighted channel letters have red returns with a 4'' depth. The red acrylic faces are illuminated with clear red neon. Incandescent light bulbs outline the face silhouetting the curve of the cabinet. Sign dimensions: Overall height — 10'x 11'-6'' wide.

Designer: Young Electric Sign Co.
Fabricator: Young Electric Sign Co.
         Ogden, UT
Client: Country Hills Plaza

Double-faced, internally illuminated 8'x10' cabinet with painted copy. Address routed through sheet metal and backed with acrylic and backlit. Pylon is fabricated with grouped wood siding laid in to form pattern and stained various colors. Complete sign is 25'0'' overall. Pylon is also lighted from below with floodlights to stand out pylon at night.

Designer: Richard Johnson/Ad-Art, Inc.
Fabricator: Ad-Art, Inc.
         Stockton, CA
Client: Cathay Hills

28' high pylon display is designed to incorporate color scheme and architectural details used in center. Copy and tenant panels are internally illuminated plastic. Pylon has architectural stucco finish over fabricated metal in sand color to match bldg. Pyramidic base element and portions of pylon use undulating ''waves'' of color relating to the surrounding, rolling desertscape.

Designer:     Communication Arts, Inc.
Fabricator:   Gordon Sign, CO
              Denver, CO
Client:       Greenwood Athletic Club

This entry sign was designed as part of an identity program which also included interior and exterior directional and identification signage for an athletic club. This internally-illuminated sign is constructed of aluminum and acrylic.

Designer:     Bob Child
Fabricator:   Gardner Signs, Inc.
              Fort Collins, CO
Client:       Vipont Pharmaceutical, Inc.

The dimensions of this sign are 14'2'' x 12'9'' x 1'11''. The cabinet is constructed with a large ''A'' extruded aluminum frame, using specially fabricated retainers to achieve the ''retainerless look.'' The faces are of ⅛'' aluminum with routed copy, backed with white acrylic for ''Pharmaceutical, Inc.'' The Vipont''

copy and logo are reversed pan-channel ''halo'' construction made of .090 aluminum faces and .063 returns. The logo and letters each have clear acrylic backs for mounting the letters to the cabinet and to prevent birds from nesting inside them. Illumination in the logo and letters is white mercury tubing; the remainder of the sign uses HO fluorescent lamps. The spiral base is constructed of 14 individual ''blades'' stacked on a common 10'' pipe through the middle of each. These ''blades'' are fabricated from .063 aluminum, finished and spot-welded together.

Designer:     Land Design-Landscape Architecture
Fabricator:   Architectural Advertising
              Ontario, CA
Client:       City of Pomona Redevelopment Agency

85' high by 35' triangular base steel tube volume
structure, acrylic spheres, polycarbonate graphics and
neon lighting, Metal halide structure lighting at Flags.

Designer: Shaw Sign & Awning, Inc.
Fabricator: Shaw Sign & Awning, Inc.
Ft. Collins, CO
Client: BMW Fort Collins

Double-faced freestanding display illuminated with daylight H.O. lamps. Extruded aluminum frame. 12'' radius corners, .080 aluminum pole cover with co-ordinating graphic stripes. Face background is painted with opaque regal blue.

Designer: Craig Neon Staff
Fabricator: Craig Neon, Inc.
Tulsa, OK
Client: Rapid Mufflers

Rapid letters are front and backlit with aluminum returns; departmental letters are front lit with aluminum returns, aluminum stripe band.

# WALL AND FASCIA SIGNS

FASCIA or WALL-MOUNTED
SIGNS are the second major
classification of sign types
identified by the sign community. As implied, this
classification of sign is
mounted or installed "flush"
against the building or facility
it identifies (as opposed to
being installed independent
of the building as are ground
signs). Wall-mounted or facia
signs share the flexibility of
fabrication materials and
methods as do ground signs,
the difference being that the
former is subject to the con-
fines of the identified building.

Designer: Ann Faulkerson and Kevin Jones
Fabricator: Jones Sign Systems
Eugene, OR
Client: Oasis

The turquoise and green border tubing and multi-color wall sign were used to enhance the building's decoration. Mimic copy, drop shadows and a black background were used for an added effect. Neon was also used inside to designate the different departments of the store.

Designer:      Graphic Solutions Ltd.
Fabricator:    Graphic Solutions Ltd.
               San Diego, CA
Client:        Judson's Restaurant

New restaurant identification (Judson's) with bare pink
neon installed over thick-and-thin script logo painted on
stucco wall; cut-out dimensional letters (Restaurant &
Galley Bar) finished with gold leaf and pale green
enamels for good day and night visibility.

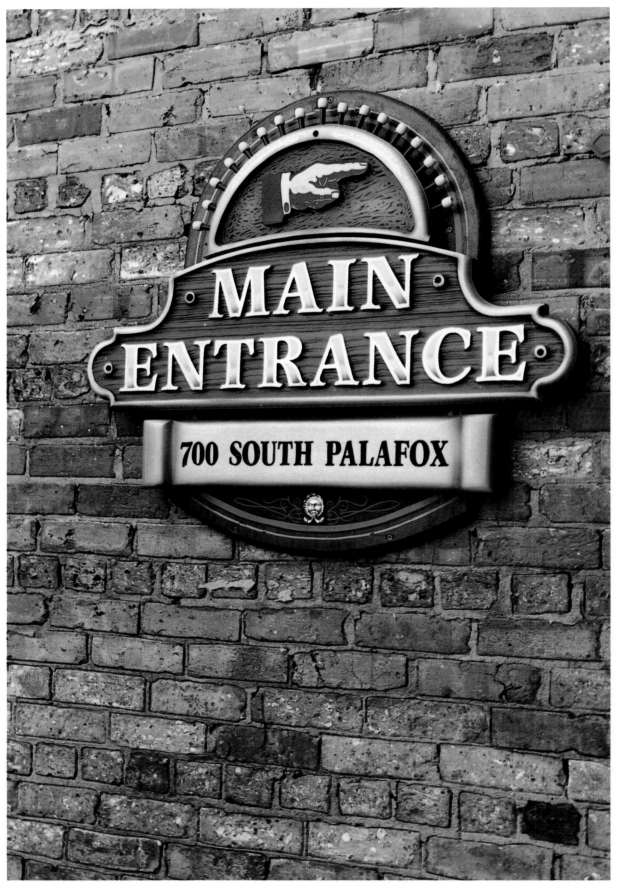

Designer: Chip Spirson
Fabricator: Vital Signs
Pensacola, FL
Client: Quayside Quarters

About 32'' x 32'' — redwood sandblasted (main ent.)

and carved (pointing finger) on MDO with tarnished brass foil border and small 22 karat gilded face — entrance sign. ''Main entrance'' is gilded with airbrush centers — address banner is carved, then sandblasted (sign company did not install).

Designer:     Ray Kinman
Fabricator:    Heartwood Signs
               San Pedro, CA
Client:       Seabreeze Apartments

Installed in lobby — handcarved Honduras magogany
3'x2'. 23K gold on ''apartments.''

Designer:     David Showalter
Fabricator:    Signs By David
               Bryan, OH
Client:       Mr. John Derks

29'' x 30'' S/F pine painted with bulletin and lettering
enamels. Goose carried a country theme with home
interior and pond.

Designer: SBG Design
Fabricator: Ad-Art, Inc.
Stockton, CA
Client: The Handlery Union Square Hotel

Elegant projecting sign and canopy consist of fab (hvy. ga.) aluminum sign case and canopy structure (painted) with routed letter-and logo openings. Push thru letters are each of unique one-piece construction — 1/2'' clear plastic triple-routed to produce finished clear letter with 3/8'' flame polished return and 1/2'' wide, 1/8'' deep shoulder/backing — all performed with cad-cam equipment. Letter faces are surfaced with rust colored 3M film, backs are spray diffused. Canopy and cabinet R/O openings are oversize, providing 1/8'' reveal all-around. Double lamping provides maximum light output thru rust film and ''halo'' outline. From exposed, flame polished letter edges. Logos are 4-piece fab. clear plastic constructions, 5'' deep, pushed thru routed openings in canopy and cabinet. Three colors of opaque (3M) film decorate faces of ''diamond'' elements, backs are spray diffused. ''Halo'' illumination defines logo shape and the ''incised'' ''H.'' Illuminated soffitt treatment (not yet installed in daytime photo, unfortunately) consists of formed white plastic (logo) panels, interior illumination. Close-up photo shows 8'6''x12' projecting sign. Canopy below measures 8'x39'6'', with 10' projection.

Designer:      Bice Adv., Inc.
Fabricator:    Geddie Neon, Windom Sign Co.
               Hattiesburg, MS
Client:        Rocket City Diner

This restaurant's 1950's theme was translated into over
300 ft. of neon using four glass colors. The logo is
repeated in two places on the facade and has border
tubing in two colors running the length of each side of
the building. The ''Diner'' lettering is backlit with neon
and made from foam board painted with black bulletin
enamel.

Designer: Mark Wessels
Fabricator: Federal Sign
Corpus Christi, TX
Client: Ole 5

The logo is fabricated aluminum reverse channel with a chrome-plated finish. Back lighting is 15mm white neon.

Designer: Chip Spirson
Fabricator: Vital Signs
Pensacola, FL
Client: City of Pensacola, FL

⅝'' thick, 9' diameter sandblasted seal on lightly tinted glass lifted into place by fork lift.

Designer: Bob Coonts / Bob Coonts Design
Fabricator: Ad Con Signs
Fort Collins, CO
Client: Leba's

Pan channel letters.

Designer: Jan McCarthy/Smith, Hinchman
& Grylls
Fabricator: Townsend Neon
Taylor, MI
Client: SH&G

Neon sign is composed of three pieces which hang from
the window mullions on the building exterior. It was
designed as the focus of SH&G's exterior Christmas
decorations for the annual citywide ''Light Up Detroit''
holiday celebration. In the building lobby, two HO model
trains — including a boxcar imprinted with bells and
holiday greeting — circle a Christmas tree and village
showcasing SH&G's clients. The train shown expands
on that theme, encircling SH&G's own building and
featuring the neon salutation on the boxcar.

Designer:     Mike & Darla Jackson, Batch & Sharon
              Anton, Raymond Chapman, Noel Weber
Fabricator:   Jackson Signs
              Jackson Hole, WY
Client:       Spirits of the West

32'' x 8'. 3/4'' M.D.O. sign with 3'' redwood millwork
on edges and corners. Background black enamel with
maroon smaltz panels 3/4'' M.D.O. with various
enamel treatments. Painted pictorial adapted from
Mucha.

Designer:     Curt Oxford Woodcarver
Fabricator:   Curt Oxford Woodcarver
              Sebastian, FL
Client:       Capt. Hirams

Logo is 48'' wide handpainted duraply floating 1'' off
the wall.

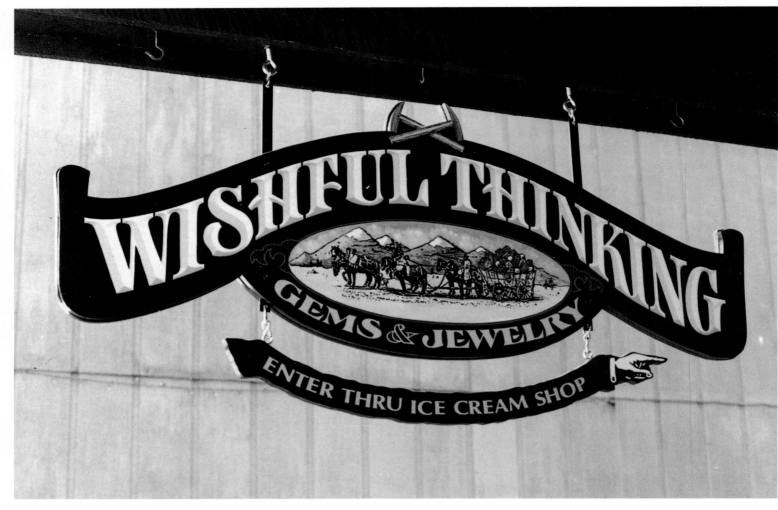

Designer: Gary Anderson
Fabricator: Bloomington Design
Bloomington, IN
Client: Wishful Thinking

Enamel on M.D.O. with silk screened pictorial and then glazed — prismatic painted letters. 2' x 4'..

Designer: Ira Spector
Fabricator: Spector Design, Inc.
San Diego, CA
Client: Rebelo

Sandblast redwood, gold leaf, deep engraved brass; stain, paint.

94

Designer: Mike & Darla Jackson
Fabricator: Jackson Signs
Jackson Hole, WY
Client: God's Own Creation

3/4'' M.D.O. with 3/4'' M.D.O. overlays. 23K gold trim. Blended prismatic effect on main copy. Airbrushed crystals. Black glass smaltz in background.

Fabricator:     Gordon Sign Company
                Denver, CO
Client:         Champa Street Minimall

The ''Champa Street'' portion of display measures
15-33'', with the ''Minimall'' bring 31'' exposed neon
channel letters — 60ma neon with remote transformers.
One tube of clear 30ma red neon border tubing
highlights the arch areas of this restored building in
downtown Denver. The transformers are remote-
mounted to sheet metal raceway behind parapet on
upper section and inside building on lower section.

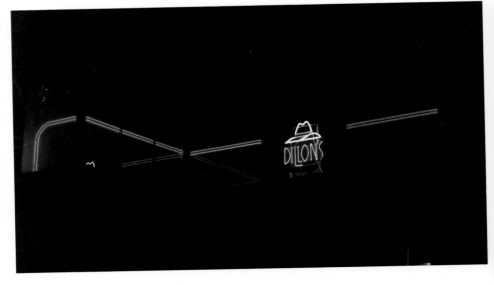

Designer:       Mr. Neon Lighting Co.
Fabricator:     Mr. Neon Lighting Co.
                Ann Arbor, MI
Client:         Dillon's

Interior exposed neon 22' in length.

Designer:    Jack Dubois / Ad-Art, Inc.
Fabricator:  Ad-Art, Inc.
             Stockton, CA
Client:      Slot Joynt Casino

24'0'' high twin ''art-deco'' style towers (surfaced with polished clear and satin-finished aluminum cladding) flank extremities of 200' frontage for this 1930's period slot casino on famed Las Vegas strip. Free-standing (roof) towers are steel structure with fabricated metal surfaced with aluminum. Accent trim and raceways are polished oak and polished gold aluminum — multi-color bands (fabricated metal with enamel finish) roll up sides of towers and out across top of continuous, backlit reader boards. Same treatment returns 50' additional on one building return. Towers are illuminated with combination ''traveling'' cerise grid neon and outlines of multi-tube gold and single tube cerise and turquoise neon. Letters are reverse channel letters, illuminated by double tube clear red neon. Chasing and scintilating 25W clear bulbs complete lighting action.

Designer:    Gary Anderson
Fabricator:   Bloomington Design
             Bloomington, IN
Client:      Finishing Touches

Enamel on M.D.O. with glazed flower arrangement.
2' x 5'.

Designer:    Susie Baggs
Fabricator:   Signs & Graphics
             Celina, OH
Client:      Celina Home Finishing Supplies

6' x 2½' with circle 2' diameter cutout. Sign was cut
out of single piece of M.D.O., then stained pine lattice
was mounted behind circle. Flower and butterfly cut out
of M.D.O., painted and mounted on lattice. Lettering
enamels used throughout and butterfly antennae are
painted nails!

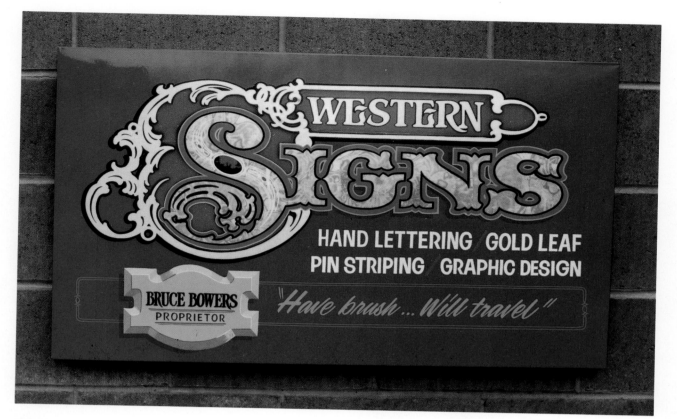

Designer: Bruce Bowers
Fabricator: Western Signs
Kenmore, NY
Client: Western Signs

42'' x 24'' F.S. / Aluminum over frame panels have airbrushed edges / ''signs'' is varigated red leaf / scrolls are 23K gold leaf. Blind mounted to building.

Designer:     Curt Oxford
Fabricator:   Curt Oxford Woodcarver
              Sebastian, FL
Client:       The Wine Seller

2'' duraply panel painted with four coats background
enamels. Letters — 23K gold leaf with light blue green
pin stripe. Bottle, grapes and glass handpainted with
airbrushed highlights.

Designer:     Gary Anderson
Fabricator:   Bloomington Design
              Bloomington, IN
Client:       Victoria's Time

Enamel on M.D.O. — 2' x 3½'.

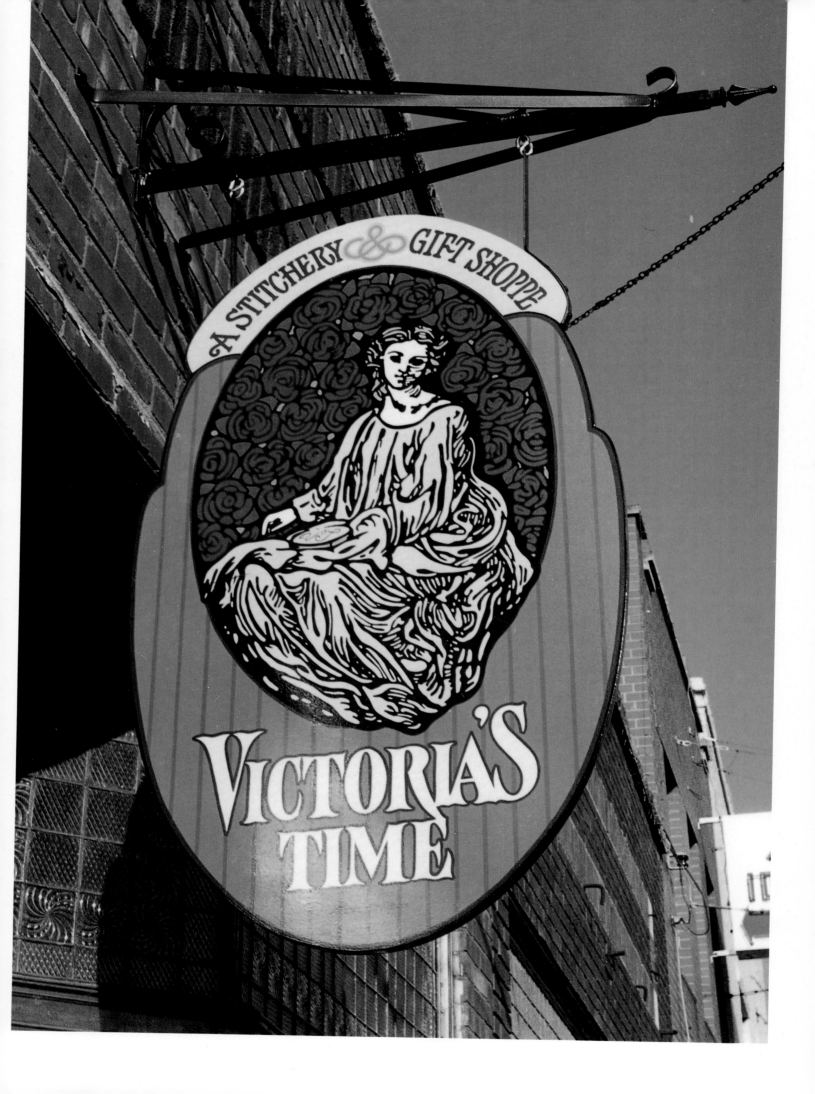

Designer:     Sign Consultants, Inc.
Fabricator:    Neon Design Inc.
                 Minneapolis, MN
Client:       Fifth Street Bootery

Exposed single-stroke neon.

Designer:     Mr. Neon Lighting Co.
Fabricator:    Mr. Neon Lighting Co.
                 Ann Arbor, MI
Client:       Brandy's

Neo-blue neon pumped with red gas. Size is approx.
20'x10' exposed neon.

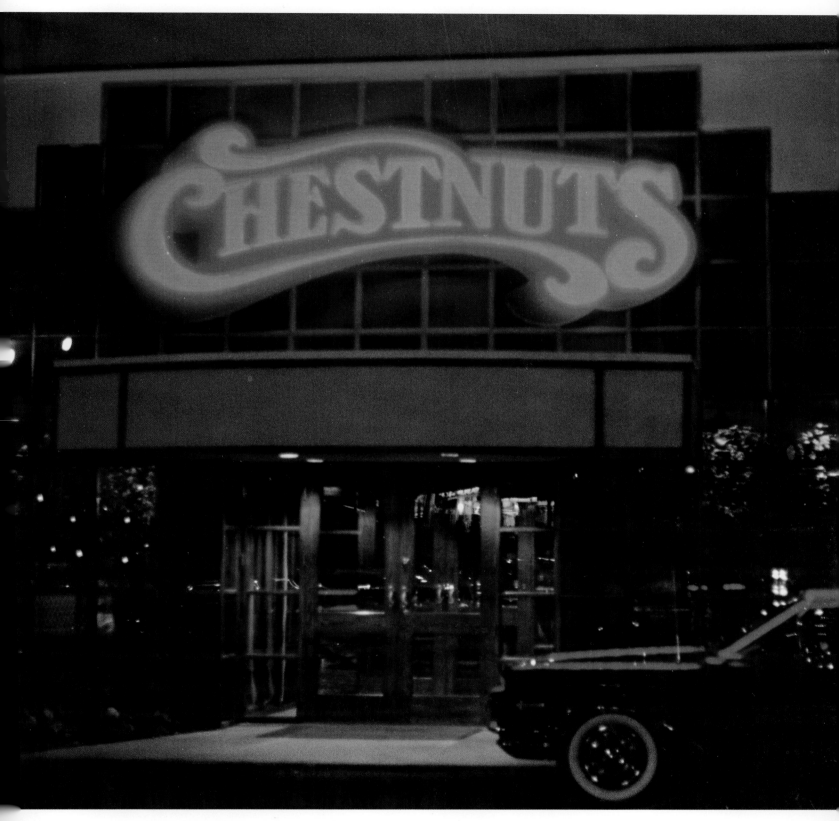

Fabricator:    Jutras Signs Inc.
                      Manchester, NH
Client:         Hospitality Holdings Corp.

6'6'' x 18' 1/2'' metal-faced plywood background with
trim cap applied to edges. Brown background sprayed
on using enamel paint. Yellow ''chestnuts'' sprayed to
background 12mm ruby red neon applied to metal-faced
plywood using clear plastic clips. (Neon outlines
letters.)

Designer:      Jones-Fortney Design & Neon
Fabricator:    Jones-Fortney Design & Neon
               Auroa, CO

This 14'x4' lobby canvas has been airbrushed and
accented with exposed neon. The bank logo is made of
acrylic, painted on the reverse and backlit. Colors are
purple, rose and aquamarine.

Designer:      Robert S. Costa
Fabricator:    Greater Pittsburgh Neon, Inc.
               Pittsburgh, PA
Client:        First City Company

$\frac{5}{8}$'' plate glass with a $\frac{3}{8}$'' etch, side-illuminated with
15mm brilliant blue neon. The city scapes are fabricated
of satin finished aluminum composite board. The
illumination between the front and rear city scapes is
accomplished with 15mm ruby red neon. The case
frame and stand-off letters are $\frac{1}{4}$'' brass, chrome plated
and mirror finished. The entire case except the frame
and letters, is set into the wall.

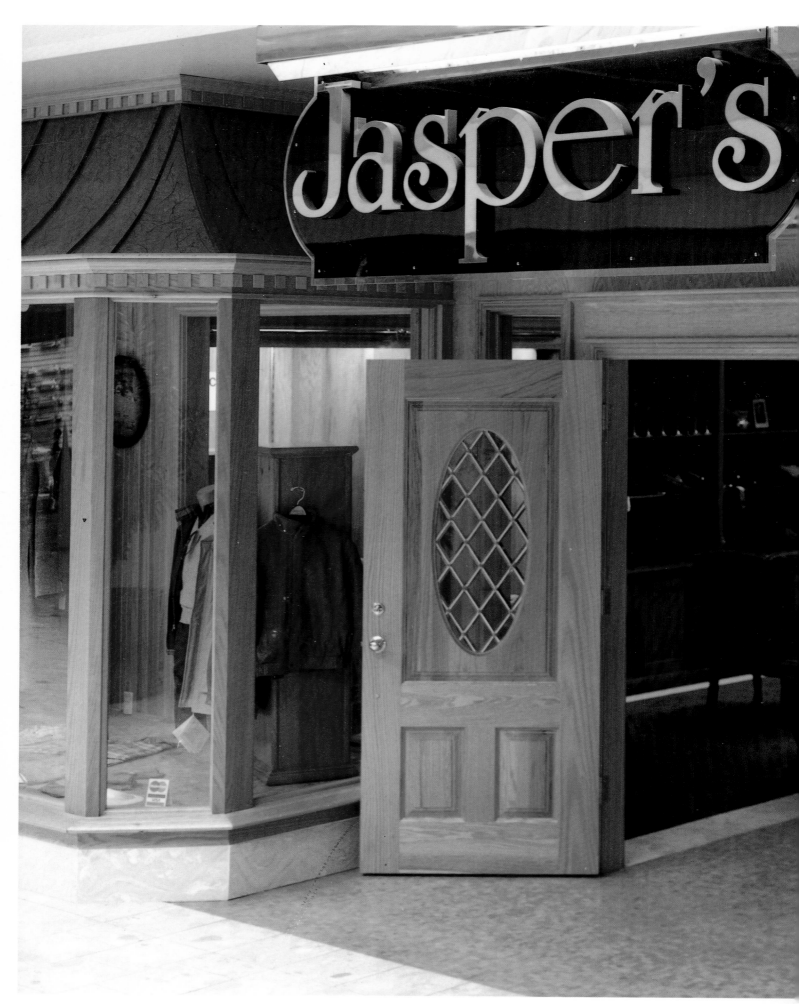

Designer:     CNI Staff
Fabricator:   Craig Neon, Inc. (CNI)
              Tulsa, OK
Client:       Jasper's

Laminated 1/4'' transparent green on each side of 1''
clear plexiglass with wood and brass laminated three
dimensional letters. Illuminated by brass fluorescent
fixture. Sign is suspended from the ceiling.

Designer: Artdev/Eloise Johnson
Fabricator: Artdev Graphics Corporation
DeLand, FL
Client: B.T. Bones

B.T. Bones is an original logo developed for a steakhouse moving into Florida. Marked channel letter faces fade from flame orange to deep red at bottom.

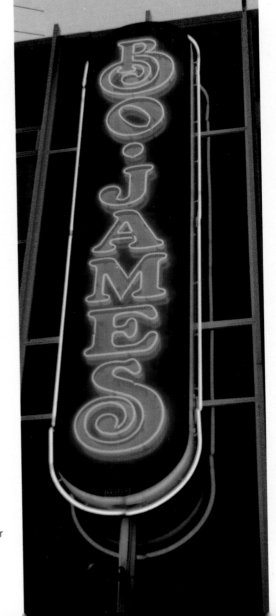

Designer: Larry Garman/Gregg Pospisil
Fabricator: Nesper Sign Advertising, Inc.
Cedar Rapids, IA
Client: Bo James Saloon

3' x 16' .080 aluminum cabinet. 15mm green border tubing; 13mm clear red letters.

Designer: Devlin Electric Sign Company, Inc.
Fabricator: Devlin Electric Sign Company, Inc.
Nanaimo, B.C., Canada
Client: Trax

This display features stylized mauve neon lettering with incandescent, illuminated dots depicting electrodes painted on acrylic discs behind a routed sheet metal face with enamel finish. ''Music-Vision'' is painted on a fluorescent illuminated acrylic panel. Clear bulbs on a three-point flasher surround display enhancing the entertainment image of this record and video store.

FLOWERS
From Everedy Square

Designer: William Cochran/The Signworks
Fabricator: The Signworks
Walkersville, MD
Client: Flowers From Everedy Square

Flat wall-mounted wood sign, about 3' x 4' is
handlettered and airbrushed. Background is blue into
green into yellow, flower is fire-red into yellow, letters
yellow into fire-red.

Designer: J.R. Haller
Fabricator: J.R. Haller Limited, Inc.
Columbus, OH
Client: J.R. Haller Limited, Inc.

2' x 2' polished yellow brass wall plaque. Coped copy
backed with 1/4'' black acrylic framed with aluminum
extrusion. Installed to Historic Building with aluminum
studs in mitre joints.

111

Designer: Thorough-Graphic Signs
Fabricator: Thorough-Graphic Signs
Lexington, KY
Client: Shumaker's, Inc.

Approx. 4'x12' MDO on 2''x4'' frame. This is a flat
sign, airbrushed and painted to look as if it were
sandblasted at about 25% of the cost.

Designer: Ron Reedy
Fabricator: Reedy Design Assoc.
Exeter, NH
Client: Isles of Shoals Steam Ship Co.

5/8'' MDO painted sign; airbrush background
(enamel); handpainted whales. Map of coast 22K gold
leaf lettering.

Designer:    Gary Anderson
Fabricator:  Bloomington Design
             Bloomington, IN
Client:      White Rabbit Card & Gift Shop

Background is enamel on MDO — applied cut-out letters
are airbrush blended.

Designer: Larry Yaekel & Assoc., AIA
Fabricator: Neon By Sklar, Inc.
San Diego, CA
Client: Chad's Rainbow

A neon display runs the full length of this storefront located in a mall. The colors used to form the rainbow border are coated ruby red, coated noviol gold and coated bromo blue. On a track in front of the neon is a functional toy train which runs the full length of the exterior, enters through the rainbow to the inside of the store, runs on a track throughout the store and exists through the opposite rainbow back to the storefront again. Inside the store are individual neon signs in coated ruby red, mounted on black acrylic.

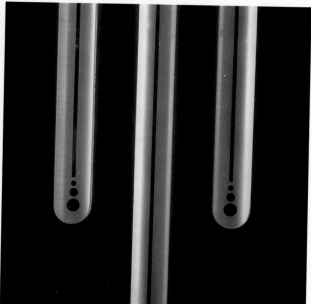

Designer:     Ron Tonelli
Fabricator:   Ferrucci Signs
              West Haven, CT
Client:       Swept Away

This 16'-wide mall storefront was fabricated from sheet aluminum and sprayed with metallic silver. The side details have reverse-etched, clear push-through acrylic backed with blue and magenta neon. The open face channel letters and raceway are suspended from the corner units.

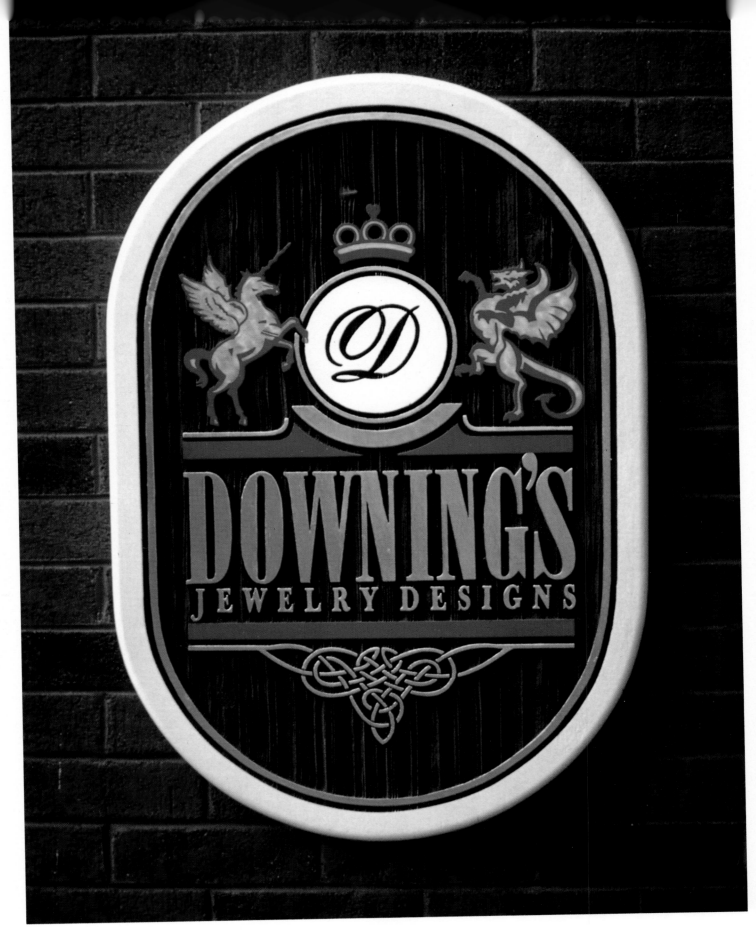

Designer: William and Nancy Cochran,
The Signworks
Fabricator: The Signworks
Walkersville, MD
Client: Downing's Jewelry Designs

Sandblasted signs with 23K gilded copy, pinstripe and
celtic knot. Spun gold on animal figures. Border is light
peach.

Designer: Back to Basics Marketing
Fabricator: Robert Bogdan Rustic Designs
Welland, Ontario, Canada
Client: Forest Heights

This sign measures 8'x3½' and is constructed of pine and cedar. The maple and oakleafs along with the keys and acorns are all hand carved. This is a new residential subdivision with 200-year-old oak trees and a new red maple planted on each lot.

Designer: William Cochran, The Signworks
Fabricator: The Signworks
Walkersville, MD
Client: Crabapples Delicatessen

Original antique pine flooring of the historic building was airbrushed with transparent oil stain in varying densities (colors) to create the design. About four feet across and located in the center of the floor. Existing flaws, cracks and stains in floor intentionally left as part of the effect.

117

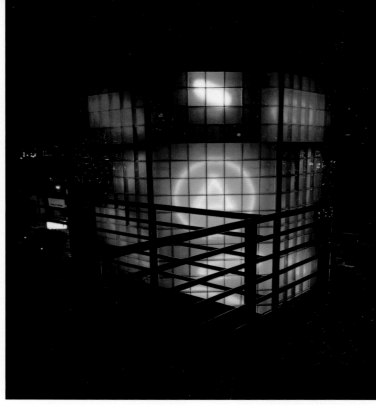

Designer: Cork Marcheschi
Fabricator: St. Elmo's
Minneapolis, MN

The approximately 1000 linear feet of neon focus on shaped reflectors with multiple custom faders, creating constant flowing change. Forms diffuse through a 32'x17'x5' deep glass-block tower on the third level of floating gardens. The piece projects southwest over downtown Des Moines, IA. The glass-block tower is free-standing.

Designer:     Cork Marcheschi
Fabricator:   St. Elmo's
              Minneapolis, MN
Client:       Actor's Threatre

Dimensions: 40'x12' on a 40' radius. Outside border
area: Indirect projected lighting from straight tubes /
color field lighting: From rectangular tubes. Center
active area: Indirect and direct lighting with random
animation by 36 electronic faders. Approximately 900'
of tubing.

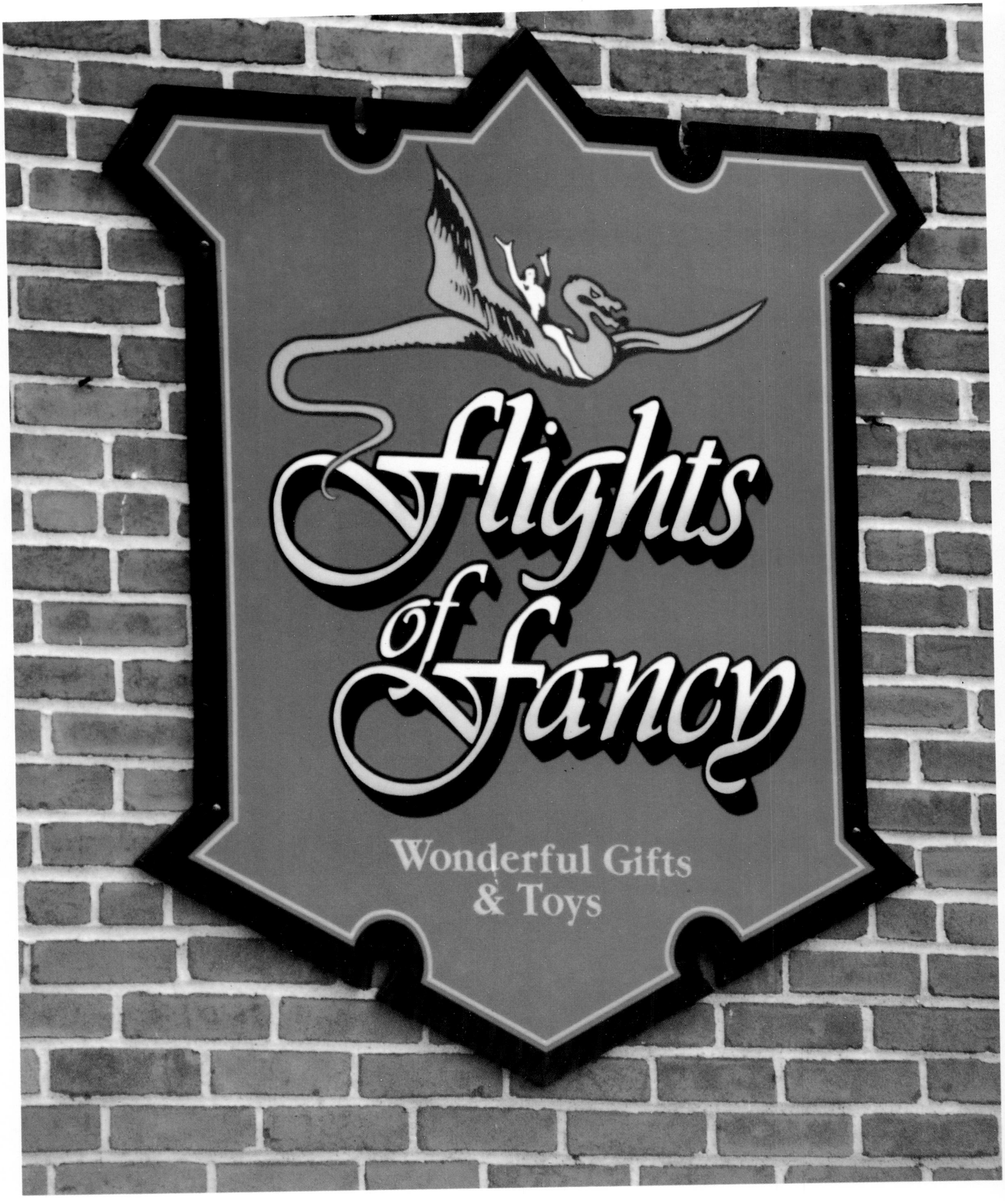

Flights of Fancy

Wonderful Gifts
& Toys

Fabricator: The Sign Man/Rick Hall
Kill Devil Hills, NC
Client: The Phoenix, Duck, NC/
Women's Fashion

Airbrushed pictorial and handlettered copy on 2' x 12'
spliced MDO, with 1'' x 4'' frame.

Designer: Ben McKnight
Fabricator: Sharper Images
Client: The Apple Branch

2' x 8' x 3/4'' MDO wall sign is mounted with 3/4''
offset. Handlettered graphics.

Designer: William Cochran/The Signworks
Adaptation of existing logo
Fabricator: The Signworks
Walkersville, MD
Client: Flights of Fancy

Handpainted wood sign is approximately 3' x 5'. Letters
are airbrush-blended white onto gold.

Designer:      Logo by client
Fabricator:    International Neon
               Montreal, Quebec, Canada
Client:        A&A

Large facade sign in metal construction with five rows of
orange exposed neon tubing and one row of white
outline. Neon with 3'' deep moulded red plastic letters.
Size 20'x45', 2600 linear feet of neon.

Designer:    HOK Graphics
Fabricator:  Zimmerman Sign Company
             Dallas, TX
Client:      Mobil Exploration & Production
             Services, Inc.

Two element sign unit; custom fabricated with painted
face and polished returns and tube reflectors
surrounded by polished stainless steel ring. Sign body
red neon stainless steel ring white neon. 21' diameter
overall.

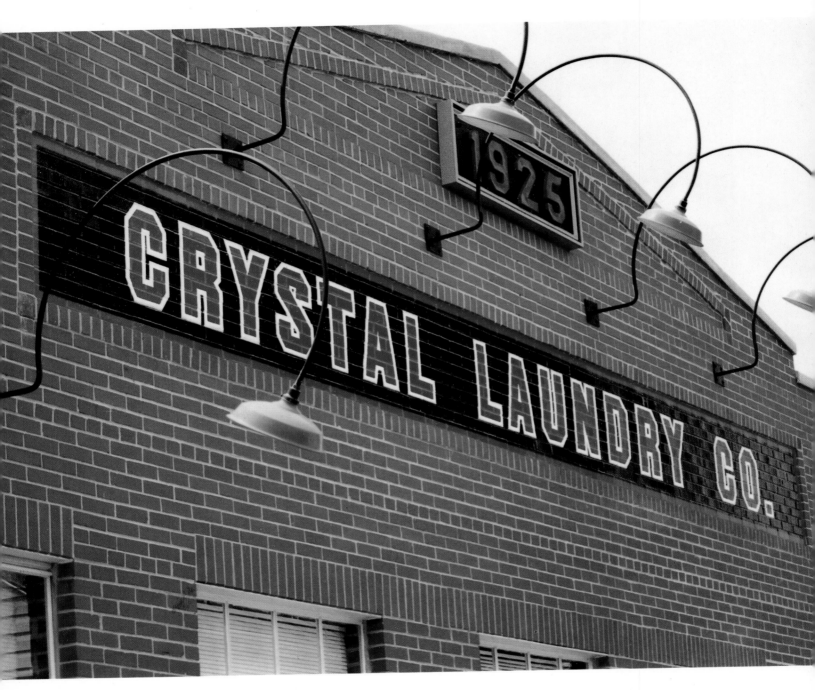

Designer: Timothy F. Crosby, architect,
Design Resource/MRO and
William M. Cochran, The Signworks
Fabricator: The Signworks
Walkersville, MD
Client: Crystal Design Center

Recreation of antique wall mural on adoptive-reuse
project building is now a design center. Handpainted on
bulletin colors on brick.

Designer: Gilmore Design
Fabricator: The Sign Company
New York, NY
Client: The Grille

Handpainted on wood panel.

Designer: Bill Hueg/Signs of Distinction
Fabricator: Signs of Distinction
St. Paul, MN
Client: Byerly's Edina Gallery

Painted marble background to match interior of store.
23K goldleaf letters with brown outline; 23K goldleaf
frame.

Designer:      Ronald E. Pomerleau
Fabricator:    Roland's Neon Sign Co. Ltd.
               Windsor, Ontario, Canada
Client:        Downtown

1'3'' x 9'6'' aluminum carrier box has backlit copy with
illuminated red acrylic channel letters fastened to face
panel.

Designer: Chic Illuminated Awnings
Fabricator: Chic
Montreal, Quebec, Canada
Client: Mazigi

As the building structure had different projections we constructed three different awnings to create the look that this optician wanted. The two outside awnings are 3' high x 15' projection. The center one is 3'x8' long. We selected an opaque background to create a subtle image he was looking for. The covering is a flexible vinyl.

Designer: Doug Euers
Fabricator: General Sign
Bloomington, IN
Client: New York Hair Design

8'x8' pan face — designed, hand cut and sprayed by Doug Euers — installed by General Sign.

Designer: Mark Oats / Dana Jones
Fabricator: Mark Oats Designs
Denver, CO
Client: Jazzercise on Capitol Hill

Irregular 82 sq. ft. relief-mounted MDO, finished in
enamels; cutout and flat-painted effects.

Designer:     Debbi Kehoe / Dana Myers
Fabricator:   Kehoe Design & Signs
Client:        Wild 'N' Woolly of Waitsfield

3'x3' overall / 3/4'' MOD — cutout shape shadowed
letters / colors on photo are true.

Designer:     Pam Swenson/Gretchen Olson
Fabricator:   Northern Lights Neon Sign Co., Inc.
             St. Paul, MN
Client:       Victoria Garden Chinese Restaurant

Located inside a mall and needed an attention-getter to let people know they existed. The sign is legible both day and night; a combination of sign painting and exposed neon. The can is 20'6'' long by 5' high. Seven tubing colors were used: clear red, green, yellow, blue, white, amber and ruby red. The flames are 3-D and protrude from the can approximately 2'.

Designer:     Karla M. Allan
Fabricator:   Young Electric Sign Co.
              Ogden, UT
Client:       Cache Valley Horseman

This 50' long x 3'6'' high exposed neon display incorporates (23) red neon graphic horses running in irregular groups across the building front, and pan-channel copy. The free standing wood pylon with molded horse and pan-channel copy display completes the western motif of the saddle, harness and tack business.

131

Designer: Wiemers-O'Connor & Partners
Fabricator: Signpost Signs, Inc.
Metairie, LA
Client: Edward J. DeBartolo Corp.

161' construction wall uses 69 sheets of MDO.
Graphics are bulletin enamel and vinyl and are designed
to match the building's architecture.

# PROJECTING SIGNS

PROJECTING SIGNS comprise the third main classification of signage. Like the facia variety, projecting signs are somewhat limited in flexibility due to their method of installation. On the other hand, projecting signs may incorporate all the various materials and techniques appropriate to facia and ground signs. This species of sign is almost a necessity for pedestrian-oriented traffic.

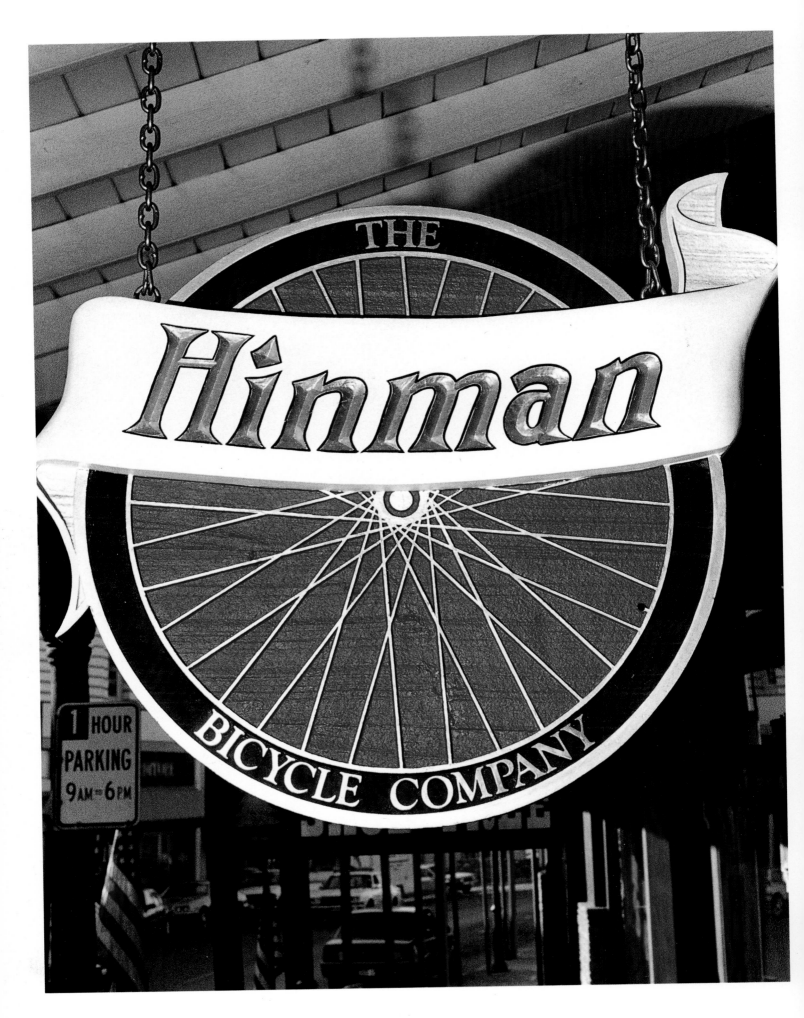

136

Designer:       Jim Hinman
Fabricator:     Len & Nickie Gorsky, Signcrafters
                Nevada City, CA
Client:         Hinman Bicycle Co.

Sandblasted and hand incised carved in old growth
sequoia redwood, 2 sides, 6'' thick through the banner.
Finished in stains, enamels, and gold leaf.

Designer:       David Schultz/LWSS
Fabricator:     Larry Weitz Sign Systems, Inc.
                Dubuque, IA
Client:         Blunt, Ellis & Loewi, Inc.

Three faced ''cube'' is installed on rounded corner of
building. Each face incorporates two internally
illuminated panels and a bar style Dow Jones display
which is controlled from offices.

Designer:     Mike & Darla Jackson
Fabricator:   Jackson Signs
               Jackson Hole, WY
Client:       Baggit

V-shaped sign over door. Oak woodwork (in house)
18''x28'' faces. 1/4 plate 23K gold burnished and 23K
matte pale gold burnished lines and roses. Red and
green glazes on flowers backed up with white gold.
Mother of pearl in corner squares. Red bronzing flower
in bolder stripes.

Designer:     Debbi Kehoe
Fabricator:   Kehoe Design & Signs
               Warren, VT
Client:       Kehoe Design & Signs /
               Murphy Vinyl Graphics

Size: 54''x42'' — mahogany — painted dark green
with two rectangles left natural and varnished to look
like inset wood. ''Signs'' is handcarved and gilded /
business names are painted pale green with a varnish
shadow. Paint brush handle is turned ash painted and
gilded / head is hand carved / copper was wound
around ferrule / paint on tip is magenta/flowers were
planted to match. ''Signs'' has a black shadow.

Designer:    Christopher Boehm
Fabricator:  Kieffer & Company, Inc.
             Sheboygan, WI
Client:      United Savings & Loan

Ornate double face clock/sign designed to fit nostalgic
building's architecture. Fabricated out of .125 aluminum
and 1/4'' plate aluminum clock face and copy are
routed out of aluminum and back with white plex. Sign
is dark bronze and metalic gold.

Designer:      Gary Anderson
Fabricator:    Bloomington Design
               Bloomington, IN
Client:        Top It Off

18''x30'' enamel on MDO — with panel carved to look
like material and enamel painting.

Designer:    Ray Kinman
Fabricator:   Heartwood Signs
            San Pedro, CA
Client:       Tina & Brian Lenzen

Hand carved — 18''x30'' — carved out of jelutong.

Designer:    Lee Pharr
Fabricator:   Jim Neal Signs
            Orlando, FL
Client:       Church Street Station

Cedar sign 36'' wide double faced with sandblasted
lattice background. Handpainted man and seafood.
Color blinds on background.

Designer:      Mark Taylor
Fabricator:    Natural Graphics, Inc.
                Houston, TX
Client:        Galleria Club

The two single-faced 10'x6'8'' signs are concrete and stucco structures with glass block sign faces. The copy and logo were sandblasted into the glass faces; the copy was painted opaque black, and the logo translucent blue/green. The logo is internally lit at the top and bottom edges with blue/green neon. The entire sign face is externally backlit with spotlights.

Designer:      Joan Mullen
Fabricator:    Orde Adv.
                Green Bay, WI
Client:        Uni Travel

This sign consists of channel letters with extended returns under the soffit, red acrylic and blue returns. It is internally illuminated.

Designer: Arch. Giuseppe Scattolin
Fabricator: Italneon
Treviso, Italy
Client: Stefanel

The internally neon-lit logo, obtained by channel letters,
is fastened to a steel drilled plate, held in a vertical
position on the front of the building by a steel pipe
system, the design of which had been specifically
studied to harmonize with the architectural style of the
environment. The sign is 18'x18'.

Designer: Charles Barnard
Fabricator: Ad-Art, Inc.
Stockton, CA
Client: Wilkes Bashford

Handcarved, gilded letters were mounted in pigmented, translucent red plastic which was then set behind routed letter openings in the fabricated aluminum cabinet. Routed openings are oversized, providing an even ''reveal'' around each letter for color accent by day, and, when illuminated at night, a distinctive neon-like halo glow. The cabinet is finished in deep bronze with dove grey bottom trim and a polished gold aluminum (sheathed) mounting bar.

# ILLUMINATED AWNINGS

ILLUMINATED or BACKLIT AWNINGS are a relatively new development, having first appeared in the Canadian/US Northwest in the late 1970's. The sign type is simultaneously "projecting" and "wall-mounted" in appearance and offers its own special set of characteristics. Particularly adaptable to strip mall identification, awnings are also finding their place in urban rehab, interior retail and franchise retail applications.

Designer: D.J. Griffen
Fabricator: Enseicom Signs, Inc.
Montreal, Quebec, Canada
Client: Encadrement Cadra

The 4'x2'x18' awning combines flexible vinyl, acrylic
and a 12mm recessed neon band.

Fabricator:    Flexart Signs Inc.
               Seattle, WA
Client:        Lynch's Market

Designer:      Tradewell Group / Flexart Signs, Inc.
Fabricator:    Flexart Signs, Inc.
               Seattle, WA
Client:        Tradewell

This facelift enabled the remodeling of 20 store locations
and gives the impression of elegance to a once outdated
store chain.

Designer: Kieffer & Co., Inc.
Fabricator: Kieffer & Co., Inc.
Park City, IL
Client: Blockbuster Videos

The awning used on this video rental store is constructed using flexible vinyl stretched over a tubular steel frame. The awning is used in conjunction with frontlighted letters. Letters - 24'' high. Lighted awnings - 3'' x 56'6''.

150

Designer:       Gene Shands
Fabricator:     Jones Sign Systems
                Eugene, OR
Client:         Sunny Market Basket /
                Front Row Video

Awning uses white and yellow flexible vinyl fabric. All copy, logos and graphic stripes are pressure sensitive vinyl and were cut using a computerized sign making machine and graphic design station. Solid white panels enclose the bottom.

Designer: David Knight (Epcon)
Fabricator: Epcon Sign Company
Great Falls, MT
Client: Lakeway Mall

Smooth flex face and sides canopy display (illum.) with painted logo, brass retainers and inserts; texture steel and sheet metal supports, smooth plex bottom. Illumination 400W mercury vapors. Canopy is 4' high by 34' long, and 8' deep.

Designer:     Craig Neon Staff
Fabricator:    Craig Neon, Inc.
               Tulsa, OK
Client:       Kendall Drugs

Backlit awning, with heat transferred graphics wrap
around building.

Designer:     Merv Eckman, Adcon Signs
Fabricator:    Adcon Signs
               Ft. Collins, CO
Client:       Sun Sport - Outpost

Interior illuminated awning — ABC extrusions system
with 22 oz. sign-o-flex fabric.

Designer:     Jack Dubois / Ad-Art, Inc.
Fabricator:    Ad-Art, Inc.
                Stockton, CA
Client:       No. 9 Fisherman's Grotto

An old, existing corrugated plastic canopy was replaced
at this world-famous fisherman's wharf (San Francisco)
site with a 100' long illuminated awning installation.
Two 15" wide x 22" deep entrance awnings have
multi-colored graphics applied by heat transfer.
Remainder of awnings are two-toned (yellow and blue
— client's colors). Slating support pipes are given
multi-color striping to enhance festive "Mediterranean"
theme desired by owner. Interior illumination of awnings
is by continuous light cases with formed white lexan
covers — at front and back. These illuminate awnings
and also provide strong downlighting for sidewalk fish
vendors below. (other signing existing).

Designer:        Bryan Scott
Fabricator:      Innovations Signs & Design
                 Beckley, WV
Client:          Patons

This 3'x3'18' backlit awning was completely spray-masked and spray-painted in the shop. The box window application required an independent frame and allows a lighted display window area. There is also a suspended egg crate soffit. The awning provided a facelift to a local 35-year-old landmark.

Designer:     Grate Signs, Inc.
Fabricator:   Grate Signs, Inc.
              Joliet, IL
Client:       Improvisation. . .

This backlit awning consists of fluorescent lighting, an
aluminum frame and vinyl covering.

Designer: Chic Illuminated Awnings
Fabricator: Chic Illuminated Awnings
Montreal, Quebec, Canada
Client: Copie Express Printing

3' high x 28' long by 3' projection awning was used together with a 3' x 20' illuminated double faced sign to draw attention to the building. The cross street is half a block away from the store and is much higher in elevation therefore the double faced sign was incorporated to draw attention using reverse colors.

Designer: Chic Illuminated Awnings
Fabricator: Chic Illuminated Awnings
Montreal, Quebec, Canada
Client: Mike's

Illuminated awnings and signs were used to create a certain look for this fast food chain on exterior of the shopping mall. A total of six exterior awnings and three wall signs were used. The overall square footage we were working with was 500 square feet and frames were covered flexible vinyl.

Designer:      Larry Gipson (in-house designer)
Fabricator:    Federal Sign Company
               Dublin, CA
Client:        Western Appliance Company

Storefront application. Fabricated in shop and installed
as a new facade. Entrance canopy and striped eyebrow
canopies are illuminated vinyl awning. Upper panels are
metal decking with pan channel letters and exposed
neon. Job was sold by using a scale model of building
in presentation.

# GLASS AND WINDOW SIGNS

GLASS/WINDOW SIGNS are a specialized category, related to facia signs in appearance, but painted or applied (as in adhesive vinyl or other films) directly to a glass surface. Typically employed in traditional storefront settings, glass signage is also being used in interior applications. The interest in "period" themes — art deco, art nouveau, Victorian, etc. — are linked with the rediscovery of such glass decoration techniques as gilding, glue chipping, sandblasting and etching, to name a few.

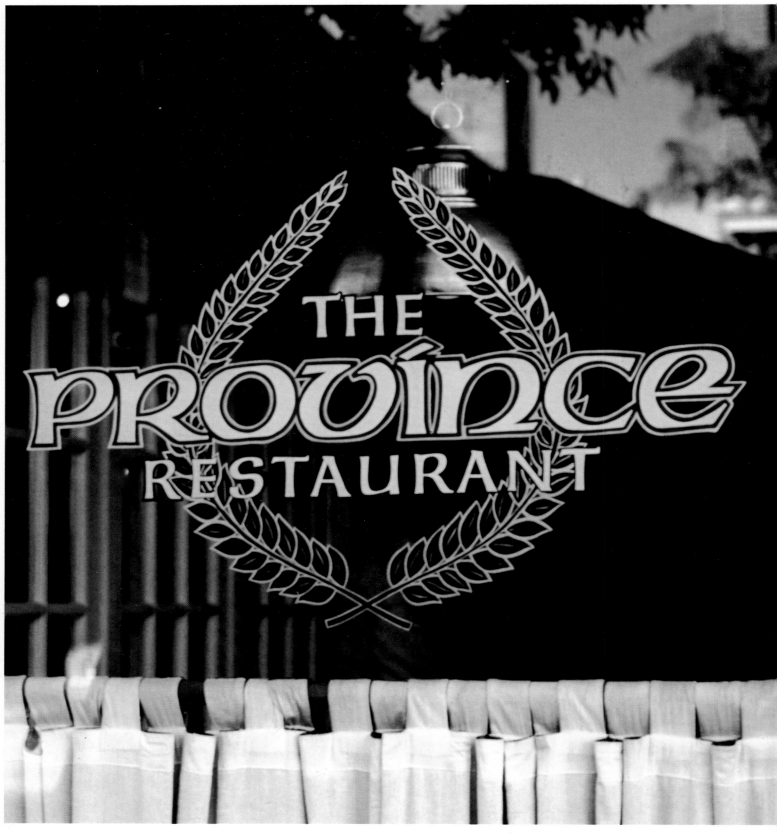

Designer:      William Cochran
Fabricator:    The Signworks
               Walkersville, MD
Client:        The Province Restaurant
Photo:         Ed Rose

Handpainted in enamels on window. Ivory letters
outlined in burgundy and gold, dark green wreath with
gold outlines. ''The'' outlined in burgundy;
''restaurant'' in dark green.

Designer:      William Cochran - The Signworks
Fabricator:    The Signworks
               Walkersville, MD
Client:        Paul's Deli

Sign company designed the logo for the business, then
handlettered it in enamels on the glass.

Designer: William Cochran - The Signworks
Fabricator: The Signworks
Walkersville, MD
Client: Quynn's Mercantile

Quynn's Mercantile is located as an adaptive-reuse project at the site of the oldest retail site in Maryland — a hardware store founded circa 1796. The hardware store used an anvil as a symbol. Window is two tone gold with split shadow of black and dark cranberry. This is the primary sign for the site. Side and rear entrance signs are sandblasted redwood with cranberry bleed, gold and ivory letters with black and teal blue split shade. Directory same, except letters are gilded. Sign at interior entrance to arcade of shops is etched glass. The two anchor tenants also have primary exterior signs. The bakery sign is two-tone gold leaf with a split shade, and the restaurant sign is electric, with custom wrought iron (cast) brackets above and below. The sign company did not do the installations, and they did not do the electrical hook-up (1) on the restaurant sign.

Designer: Potions and Lotions (client)
Fabricator: Watermark
Philomath, OR
Client: Potions and Lotions

Screen printed on glass in three locations, ''gilded''
with aluminum leaf, glitter, hand lettered. 24'' x 24''
plus lettering.

Designer: Terry Kid
Fabricator: Kid Sign Co.
West Allis, WI
Client: Kid Sign Co.

Varigated gold border and brush ''kid'' gold border with
matte center. Handpainted green leaf effect on office
door. Transparent orange vinyl inside circle.

Designer: William M. Cochran / The Signworks
Includes adaptation of antique pictoral
from the Dover Archive series.
Fabricator: The Signworks
Walkersville, MD
Client: Sir Thomas Catering

Handlettered in enamels — gold detail is bronze paint
(permageled). Pictorial is adapted from 19th century line
drawing. Grey letters with burgundy and charcoal gray
split shade — picture in white, silver, burgundy, gold
and blue-grey.

164

Designer:    Liza Metzley
Fabricator:  Signs by Liza
             Naperville, IL
Client:      Antique Bazaar

Olive chipped plate glass 23K gold, handpainted marble.
Background approx. size 18''.

Designer:    William M. Cochran of The Signworks
             with an illustration by Don Cleavland
Fabricator:  The Signworks
             Walkersville, MD
Client:      Beneath It All
Photo:       Ed Rose

Lingerie shop in historic district — done on front
window — handlettered and airbrushed in enamels
(rose, burgundy, charcoal grey, cream, etc., gold is
bronze paint). Shop was so successful had to expand to
another space in eight months. Cut sign out of window,
framed it and took with them — ergo second picture.

Designer: Jay Cooke, Mike Jackson
Fabricator: Jay Cooke's Sign Shop
Stowe, VT
Client: Stowe Flake Resort

Winfield's has a pale gold burled matte center — with a dark green outline. Illustration is airbrushed, burnished and matte gold outline, dark green border design. Charlie B's is 23K gold airbrushed matte center. Both have the snowflake in white gold. The facade's color scheme was then designed to compliment windows. Panels approx. 6'x6'.

Designer:     Richard Mech
Fabricator:    Sherlick Incorporated
                Lockport, IL
Client:       Sherick Incorporated

The 82'' x 77'' oak doors were fabricated in-house and inset with custom designed windows which were sand-blasted, glue chipped, and overlayed in gold-leaf. The handles were also custom designed to match our logo and then brass-plated.

Designer: William M. Cochran / The Signworks Includes adaptation of antique pictoral from the Dover Archive series.
Fabricator: The Signworks Walkersville, MD
Client: Victorian Spirits & Wine Boutique

All lettering 23K gold — including rim of circle. All else handlettered in enamels. Pictorial adapted from detail of 19th century line drawing. Green frog, burgundy morning coat, white shirt, grey pants, ivory background.

Designer: Noel B. Weber, Sign Painter
Fabricator: Noel B. Weber
Boise, ID
Client: Andrus Shane

Sign is 18K gold leaf centers with 23K gold outlines. Logo panels is 23K gold outlines with 18K gold centers on a green toned marble background.

Designer:       David Estes
Fabricator:     Eagle Sign Crafters
                Anna, IL
Client:         1st National Bank of Grandtower

Restoration of old look to this bank inside and out
prompted the owner to call for these foil looking letters
in gold leaf.

Designer:       J.J. Shaw/Patty Morris
Fabricator:     Shaw Sign & Awning, Inc.
                Fort Collins, CO
Client:         Old Town Flower Market

Stained glass display. Border lighting by 13mm rose
neon. Frame of golden oak, with a clear finish.

Designer:     G. Garnett Neon design
Fabricator:   American Neon & Electric Sign Co.
              Fort Worth, TX
Client:       Fort Worth, TX

42''x96'' clear acrylic mount with 04 red neon.
''Texas'' is raised trimcapped acrylic with 6500 white
backlight. (Photo does not show installation).

Designer:     James Valley, William Masisak
Fabricator:   H&R Neon Service
              Pittsburgh, PA
Client:       The Neon Macan

This window display incorporates vivid colors to capture
the exotic nature of the image. The lettering is neon and
blue with the logo using uncoated ruby, 3500ºK white,
noviol, blue, neo blue, uncoated bromo blue, turquoise,
and coated apple green glass.

171

# INTERIOR SIGNS

INTERIOR SIGNS is a classification unto itself, and could be divided into the same three main categories of exterior described as "ground" (free-standing), facia or wall-mounted and projecting. More often than not, interior signs are designed as a "system" with a singular and identifiable "look" or theme. Interior signs have all of the flexibility of materials and fabrication methods inherent to exterior signs, but offer even more options since they are not subject to the elements.

Designer:        Randall Boone Signage, Lighting &
                 Crane Rental
Fabricator:      Randall Boone Signage, Lighting &
                 Crane Rental
                 Dana Point, CA
Client:          Polar International

Fully self contained, 5' neon bear, 75/20 core and coil
transformers, sheet metal cabinet, using ruby red neon
for the glasses and spoon, alligator is emerald green,
standard colors for remaining designs, 3/16'' clear plex
used to cover bear to prevent damage. Neon blue neon
for strip lighting, to give off the effect of being on the
north pole.

Designer:     Terry Oestreicher
Fabricator:   Neon Neon
              San Francisco, CA
Client:       The Daily Planet
Photo:        Peter MxCandless

White plexiglass cut-outs back-lit (rings and planet),
drop shadow line is turquoise neon, also white neon
outline; mounted cn painted flex surface; painted letters
(lower left corner), clear plex cover protects and has
turquoise outline of printed letters (lower left).

Designer:     Jan Paul Carter / Los Angeles Neon
Fabricator:   Los Angeles Neon
              Santa Monica, CA
Client:       Griffith Observatory, City of Los Angeles

Neon on sheet metal dimensional sign can. The sign can
is cut to form the shape and architectural style of the
building, which is a landmark of Los Angeles. The sign
can is also airbrushed to accentuate the design. The
comet above the observatory animates in pastel neon.
Approximate size: 5'x4'.

Designer:     Cage Custom Neon
Fabricator:    Cage Custom Neon
               Colorado Springs, CO
Client:       Gables Night Club

Picture 1 & 2, overall view of night club. Picture 3, note neatness of hardware. Tube supports and housings were installed prior to the spraying of the texture and paint to blend in with background .15mm purple was 1½'' from ceiling and 15mm magenta was 3'' from ceiling to give a 3-dimensional effect.

Designer:     Ben Livingston, Franklin Roberts
Fabricator:    Beneon
Client:       Self Promo

14'x40' skeleton neon/controversial issue as animated through sequences by designing and using a childs perspective of armegeddon using 11 stage sequentially controlled computer animater designed and built from scratch by Franklin Roberts specifically for this project — was used for grand opening.

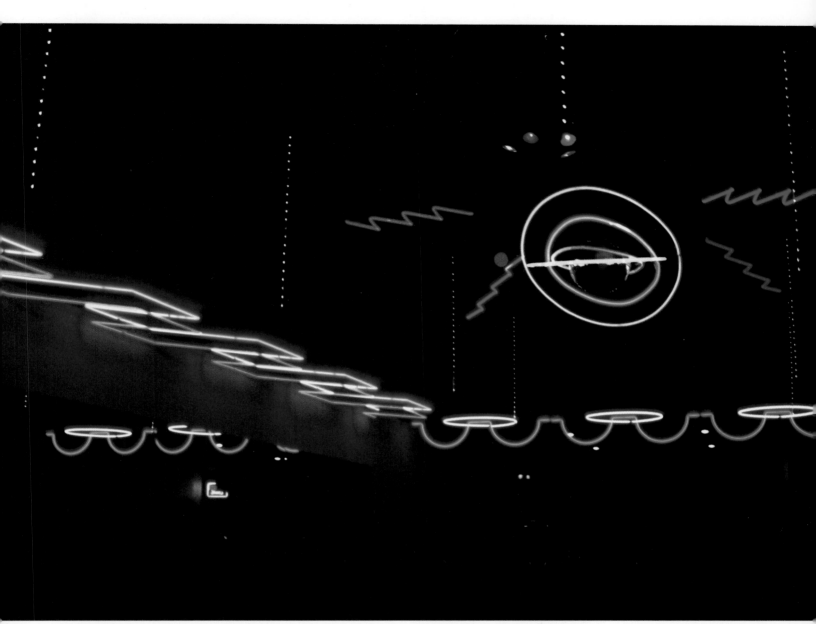

Designer:    Bruce F. Smith
Fabricator:  'Lumination's Neon
             San Francisco, CA
Client:      Western Exhibitors, Inc.

Aluminum cityscape, neon thermal-formed plexi-steel-women high heels (Bannana's) enamel paint - various found objects.

Designer:      Anne Ashley
Fabricator:    A. Ashley, Inc.
               Austin, TX
Client:        Recats International

The sculpture for the entrance lobby contains rare
glasses. . . 25mm ruby, cobalt and uranium. The 1''
thick beveled and polished acrylic piece duplicates
architectural detailing on the building 12'x16'.

Designer: Greg Dolnick
Fabricator: The Electric Art Co.
St. Louis, MO
Client: Temperature Rising

Front face of design is high-gloss black formica with
grid pattern, clear red and white neon. Recessed light
blue neon around edge of back, emits unusual glow/
indirect lighting on wall. Constructed of ABS plastic,
formica, neon, and core and coil transformer. Design is
fully encased and can be hung on a wall with one nail.
Size 23'' ea. side. Triangle, 4'' depth.

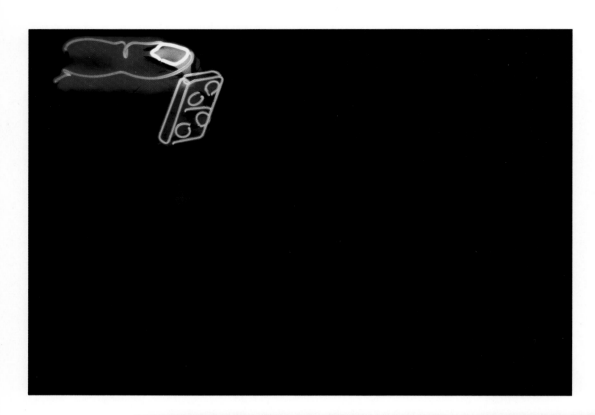

Designer:      Ben Livingston, D.C. Bisig
Fabricator:    Beneon Company
               Austin, TX
Client:        North Forty Night Club

Six stage sequentually animated neon (skeleton) staging
simulation of toppling dominos as pushed over by
finger. Display measures 5'x7'.

Designer:    Sharon Worrell
Fabricator:  Texas Sign Source
             Dallas, TX
Client:      Sound Warehouse

CD's — Sign cabinet is fabricated from 22 gauge sheet metal with automotive acrylic enamel finish. Face is 1/4'' thick mirrored acrylic. CD's copy is flat cut clear red acrylic. Multi colored neon rings flash on from outermost to innermost ring until all units are lighted. Solid state flasher and European acrylic tube supports are utilized.

TAPES — Sign cabinet is fabricated from 22 gauge sheet metal with automotive acrylic enamel finish. Face is 1/4'' thick mirrored acrylic, with clear blue acrylic strips and clear red acrylic trimcapped TAPES. Smoked acrylic ''windows'' in face and bottom cover incandescent lamps that flash at random. European designed tube supports are utilized for their modern uncluttered look.

Designer:    Patrick Bresette
Fabricator:   Graphic Light-Custom Neon
               Bastrop, TX
Client:      Westfield Realty

This neon installation was commissioned by Westfield
Realty in Rosslyn, VA and was designed by Patrick
Bresette specifically for the lobby. Special acrylic
hangers were designed and fabricated to hang the
tubing and create its 3-dimensionality. The circles and
star pattern are on a random generated sequencer and
wave dimmer to create a constantly changing visual
experience.

Designer: Carol Billman/Will Norman
Fabricator: Blue Wave Neon, Inc.
Landenberg, PA
Client: E.I. DuPont de Nemours & Co.

4'x7' neon mural hangs in reception area of DuPont's
Corporate Computer Education Center, Nemours
Building, Wilmington, DE. Materials: turquoise and
orchid exposed tubing, peach tubing for backlighting;
keyboard crafted of composite materials on urethane
foam (for raised keys); DuPont Imron® finish. Mural has
been adopted in Ed Center publications.

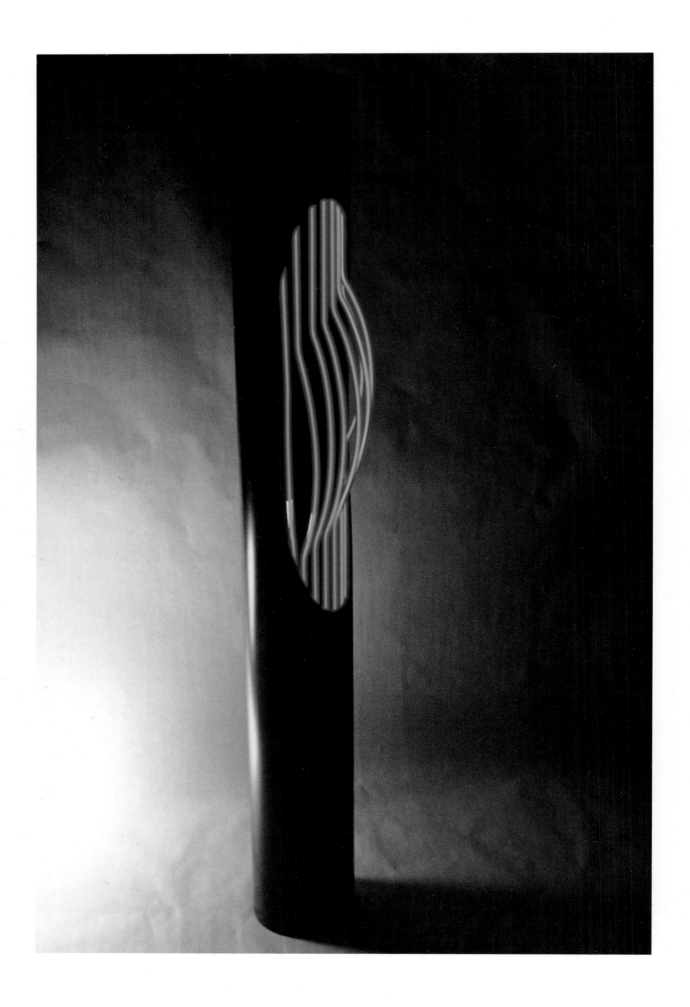

Designer:      Dhiru Thadani
Fabricator:    Light 'n Up Neon
               Washington, DC
Client:        Private Residence

Custom neon sculpture/lighting for kitchen in private residence.

Designer:      Hank Gatewood Art & Design
Fabricator:    Hank Gatewood Art & Design
               Tyler, TX
Client:        Lumbley, Swanson & Mullins, Inc.

Temporary hanging neon installation incorporated into centerpiece (floral centerpiece by Stuart Axelson, Dallas) at opening of Dallas Contract Design Center.

Designer:      Lajos Da Re
Fabricator:    Meyer Sign Co.
               Seattle, WA
Client:        Decorum

''Pregnancy'' PVC pipe 1'' diameter painted black. 12mm clear glass pumped blue and red gas. No mercury. 5' high.

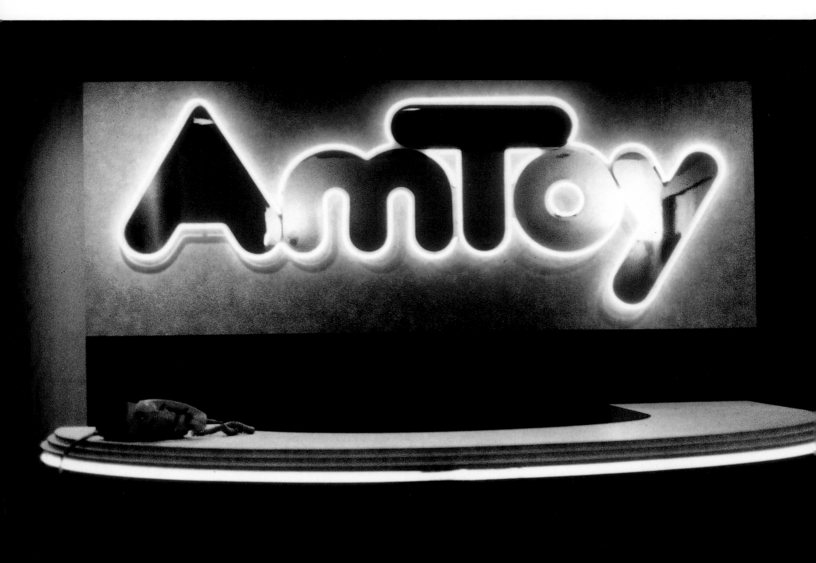

Designer: Pacifico A. Palumbo with
Exhibit Group
Fabricator: Say It In Neon, Inc.
New York City, NY
Client: LJN Toys

Formica background. Stainless steel relief letters and
neon outline of letters. Desk: Formica containing neon in
cove color (ice blue).

Designer:     Thorough-Graphic Signs
Fabricator:    Thorough-Graphic Signs
                Lexington, KY
Client:       Saffron

All elements except thin background board (1/8''
masonite) are foam. This sign is positioned behind the
counter of a elegant women's store and is subtly
painted to match wall and moulding. All cut out on hot
wire (except masonite). Size approximately 30'' x 36''.

Designer:     Douglas Coccaro
Fabricator:   C&C Westchester Sign &
              Lighting Corp.
Client:       Liberty

Exposed neon mounted on a plastic cut-out face with
backsprayed sky and lettering. Illumination with
fluorescents from within. Fabricated aluminum box with
mirrored edging. Location: Galleria Mall, White Plains,
NY. Size: 5'6''x5'.

Designer: Robert Randazzo/Absolutely Neon
Fabricator: Absolutely Neon
Albuquerque, NM
Client: Life Trends Fitness and
Rehabilation Control

Decorative neon lighting installed over 60' pool and adjacent jacuzzi area. Designed in ''Memphis style'' using standard as well as voltauc rame tubes. All wiring is concealed in the ceiling (to code). Throne is approximately 250' of tubing in chanell (open) enclosure. A similar installation is also in their work out room (downstairs area).

Designer:      Flexart Signs Inc.
Fabricator:    Flexart Signs Inc.
               Seattle, WA
Client:        Southland Corporation / 7-11

This continuous canopy directs the flow of customers to the merchandise and gives the customer comfort in a scaled down surrounding.

Designer: Dan Cline & Associates
Fabricator: Columbus Sign Company
Columbus, OH
Client: The Steak Escape

Main signs — exposed neon mounted to plex.
Secondary signs (i.e., order here / fries & drinks only)
reverse sandblasted redwood-painted menu boards —
oak framing — silkscreened plex panels.

# ARCHITECTURAL SIGN SYSTEMS

ARCHITECTURAL SIGN SYSTEMS is an all-inclusive classification comprising both interior and exterior signs in all their varieties, but distinguished (as described in ''interior signs'') from other multiple groupings of signs by their unity of design. Office parks, hospitals and airports are typical of the type of sign user in need of an architectural sign system.

Designer: Phillips Engeuge / RTKL Associates
Fabricator: Belginger Sign Company
Baumore, MD
Client: JMB Federated Realty

Signs were formed aluminum neon interway illuminated boxes and exposed marquee lights.

Princeton
Market Fair

Princeton Market Fair!

Designer: Communication Arts Inc.
Fabricator: Gordon Sign Co.
Denver, CO
Client: Rivercenter

The materials used in the Rivercenter signage were
painted aluminum, sheetmetal and formed acrylic. A rich
palette of traditional and regional colors were used with
fiesta-inspired forms in response to the strong ethnic
nature of San Antonio

Designer:     Communication Arts, Inc.
Fabricator:   Nordquist Sign Co.
              Minneapolis, MN
Client:       Bayside Marketplace

Bayside Marketplace and approximately 20 sign types, including specialty area identity and the design of the Pier 5 merchandising system. Neon, metal plate and perforated metal were used extensively throughout the project. Dimensional 12' high project identity letters change from opaque, gradated color forms by day to juke-box-like objects at night. The environmental graphics combined ingredients of the Caribbean with the resort history of Miami.

205

Designer:       Sullivan & Perkins
Fabricator:     Federal Sign
                Arlington, TX
Client:         Bon Fete on the River

The sign system is a combination of neon, acrylic,
wood, aluminum and color, designed to represent the
festive atmosphere of New Orleans.

Designer: Christina Weber, Robert Gnagey /
Weber Design
Fabricator: Interior: Sign Systems, Inc.
Exterior: Gordon Sign
Client: Lew Stevens, Healthy Habits Restaurant

Dimensional logo. Mounted on exterior of building at
entry doors (4 places) to enhance and identify the entry
area. Approximately 1'6'' square. Two layers of cut and
painted acrylic with a vacuum formed hemisphere.

Entry area showing detached PVC columns, dimensional
logos (4 places) and roof top pyramid with aluminum
flag; all intended to enhance and identify the entry area.

Designer: Communication Arts Inc.
Fabricator: Nordquist Sign Co.
Minneapolis, MN
Client: Promenade

Materials used in this sign system were painted
aluminum and sheetmetal acrylic and neon. Interior and
exterior identification and directional signs were created
and include major animated neon signage with the
''Campus Level'' and ''Picnic'' signs.

Designer:     Bob Brackenbury, Federal Sign &
                   H.L. Berger/Roger Brown, Law
                   Kingdon, Inc.
Fabricator:   Federal Sign
                   Kansas City, MO
Client:        Melvin Simon & Associates, Inc.

Interior and exterior mall signage, including D.F. free-
standing signs, entry graphics and area identification
techniques include routed letters, channel letters,
stainless steel logo with neon detail, cut out 2'' clear
acrylic logos and skeletal neon lettering.

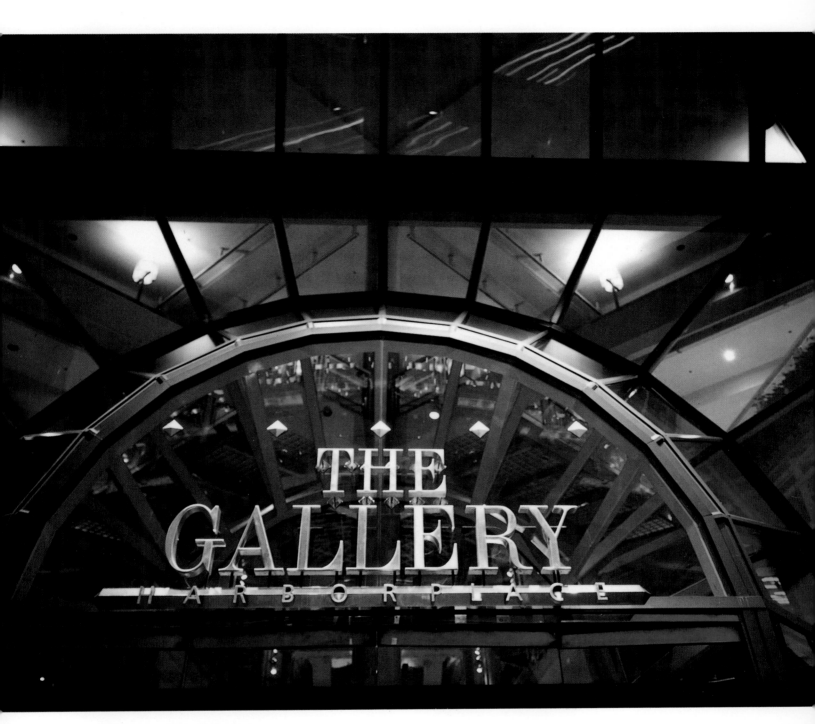

Designer: Communication Arts Inc.
Fabricator: Nordquist Sign Co.
Minneapolis, MN
Client: The Gallery

Mahogany, bronze and glass were used extensively
throughout The Gallery at Harborplace, along with
handcarved and gilded copy. The directory used edge-lit
''floating'' directory graphics at four levels within the
directory cabinet, which illuminates the graphics without
a glare.

216

Designer: Follis Design
Fabricator: Nuart Signmakers
Santa Ana, CA
Client: Rancon Realty Development

All signs are fabricated aluminum. 38'x8' triangular pylon sign has routed copy with push thru plastic letters. Sign is internally illuminated. Sister sign reading Tri City Corporate Centre is fabricated aluminum 8' letters mounted on a stucco finish raceway base. Copy Corporate Center is 1/4'' cut out aluminum letters. Sign letters are illuminated with 24' of billboard lighting fixtures. Secondary and directional signs are with routed copy, 800ma internal lighting.

Designer:     Ken Young / Ad-Art, Inc.
Fabricator:   Ad-Art, Inc.
              Stockton, CA
Client:       Oil Changers

Variety of sign component applications marks this
effective sign system. Sign variants include low-profile
monument and free-standing pylons, fascia lettering and
logo signs. Wherever logo appears, white ''oil drop'' is
''bubble-formed'' to be dimensional. Faces of
monument and pylon signs are routed aluminum with
graphics formed/decorated second surface on clear
lexan, then mechanically fastened behind face with
concealed fasteners. Fabricated aluminum cabinets and
metal supports are finished to harmonize with building
colors with polished clear aluminum trim. Fascia
displays are self-contained ''unit'' signs. Lettering and
logo signs have formed lexan faces (with trim gap
formed integrally) providing a gap effect over jig-
fabricated sign cases. Interior illumination is by
fluorescent lamps on all sign components.

Designer: D.I. Design Consultants
Fabricator: Nordquist Sign Co.
Client: Galtier Plaza

Exterior logo signage (2) is exposed neon and fluorescent/aluminum open channel construction. Interior directional signage is aluminum cabinets with acrylic faces. Tenant I.D. signs are solid brass frames with panel furnished by tenant (panels in photos done by Nordquist) 55 total. Five illuminated directories.

Designer:     Clear Communications
Fabricator:   Clear Communications
              San Marcos, CA
Client:       San Clemente Cove

Integrated sign system in tile, sandblasted, inlaid in
stucco surfaces.

Designer: Seitz, Yamamoto & Moss Inc.
Fabricator: Cook Sign Company
Fargo, ND
Client: Merit Care / St. Lukes Hospitals /
Fargo Clinic

Sign built with angle iron frame. ''Inside sign face of white acrylic plastic with custom colored vinyl letters on first surface. ''Outside'' sign face of cold formed clear lexan, sign skin of aluminum shut with sandblasted grid pattern. Lighting by flourescent lamps with red neon ''halo'' around top.

Designer:      Heinz Prosch & Associates Designs Inc.
Fabricator:    Alpha Neon
               Coquitlam, B.C., Canada
Client:        Expo 86

Custom designed typestyle — remote transformers —
single tube red neon on plymetal cut out letters fastened
to steel pipes.

Designer:      Muhlhausen Design & Associated
Fabricator:     Design Systems
                 Greensboro, NC
Client:         Marriott Marquis Hotel

Letters are custom fabricated from sheet brass. The
letter style was the hotel's logo type. Letters are 6''
deep. The faces are finished in fine satin natural brass
with two (2) coats of clear. The returns are finished in
special red enamel. Letters are installed with concealed
threaded rods.

The Garden Lounge. Sign is fabricated from solid ½''
thick brass. The shape is like a plan view of a grand
piano. The copy and roses are deep etched and paint
filled. The keyboard is sandblasted. The brass sign is
mounted on 1¼'' thick plexiglass support kiosk with
polished bullnose edge. This is mounted to (2) solid
brass support posts embedded in floor.

Pompano's. Sign is fabricated from solid 2'' thick
hardrock northern maple. The copy and logo are hand
carved into the maple. The logo was carved 1¼'' deep.
The small letters are ½'' high in Friz Quadrata style
with a ''V'' vevel. The maple received a fifteen step
walnut finish. All copy was filled with 24 karat gold leaf.
The sign is mounted using two (2) special fabricated
half round brass posts.

The base is fabricated from ⅛'' thick brass. The top of
the unit is covered with ¼'' thick brass plate. The sign
is installed using concealed mounting rods embedded in
floor.

Designer:      Larry Gipson / Federal Sign
Fabricator:    Federal Sign
               Dublin, CA
Client:        Safeway Stores Inc.

Store interior, departmental identification displays.
Installed on soffit/fascia above product areas. Displays
are continuous script (''McGuffey'' style developed by
L. Gipson) skeleton tubing set-off acrylic plastic back-
panel in relayed color neon/back panel for reflective
image. Also used over product finishing mural
''fisherman's wharf''.

Designer:     Christian Soltendieck/
              Steve Elkins/Joe Dill
Fabricator:   Flexart Signs Inc.
Client:       Ennens Foods

This entire remodeled strip center accessed many
mediums of materials. The major tenent on the outside
started with individual illuminated letters along with a
45' clock tower, a focal point from the near by interstate
highway. The rest of the center used a canopy system
with a sheet metal roof, a continuous translucent fabric
sign face along with a continuous mesh soffit panel and
internal gutter system. The major tenant's interior
package was accomplished by using a variety of
materials from eradicatable fabric for the meat and
movies awning, to a combination of mirror plex, neon,
transluscent fabric, mesh, accented with a stuffed
marlin, to simple scoteal film on transluscent fabric for
the deli.

Designer:      Kim Lluender
Fabricator:    Kluender Sign Works, Inc.
               Hastings, MN
Client:        Foodtown Diner/The Clark Group

Over 700 ft. of neon running from new exterior marquee
to interior ceiling flowing around restaurant. Assorted
small neon information signs i.e., bar, bakery,
restrooms, and logo.

Designer:      Kieffer of Illinois, Inc.
Fabricator:     Kieffer of Illinois, Inc.
               Park City, IL
Client:      First Midwest Bank

# MISCELLANEOUS SIGNS

Here we show the diversity of work that sign companies and design firms are handling these days. This MISCEL-LANEOUS chapter contains a few examples of the advertising community's reliance upon the sign trade. The most visible applications are the graphic displays. There are hundreds of companies in the trade which now deal exclusively in these burgeoning industries.

Designer:      Rick Czebiniak
Fabricator:   American Neon
              Austin, TX
Client:       Scarecrow

Designer:      Chip Gross
Fabricator:   Artech Neon Inc./Chip Gross
              Miami, FL

An almost full-sized  7'x4' overall — Harley Davidson,
this piece consists of 144' of neon.

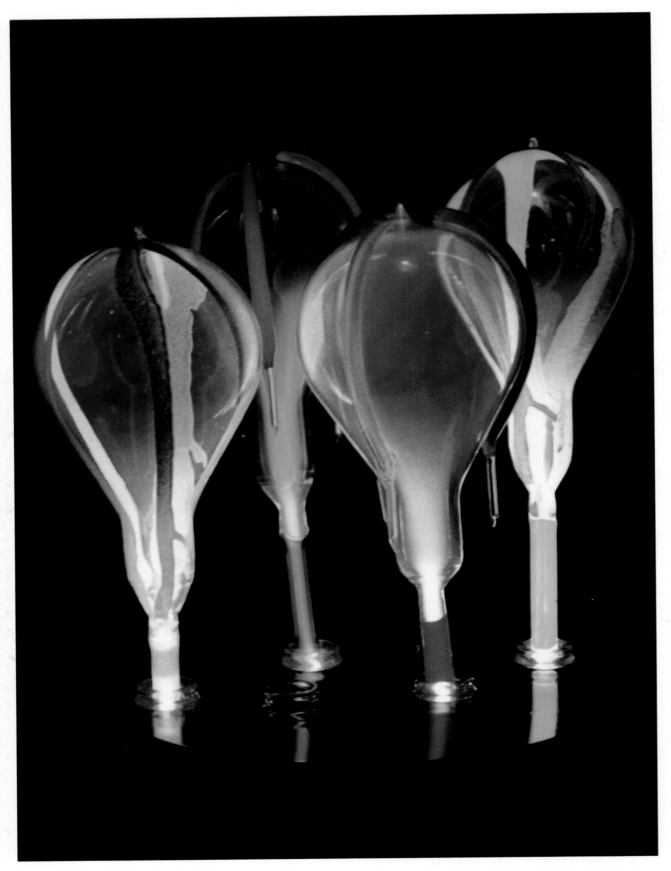

Designer:  Michael Blazek
Fabricator:  Western Neon, Inc.
      Seattle, WA

These four rare gas cylinders filled with neon and argon gas are entitled ''Hot Air Balloon Race.'' Two cylinders have had phosphors hand applied to add white, green, blue and pink tones. Two cylinders have had gas-filled tubes siliconed to the outside surface. The tubes have no electrodes attached. The cylinders, which have only one electrode each, are illuminated by a solid state transformer. The tubes attached to the cylinders illuminate by contact with a radio frequency that is generated because the transformer is not wired up ''in series.''

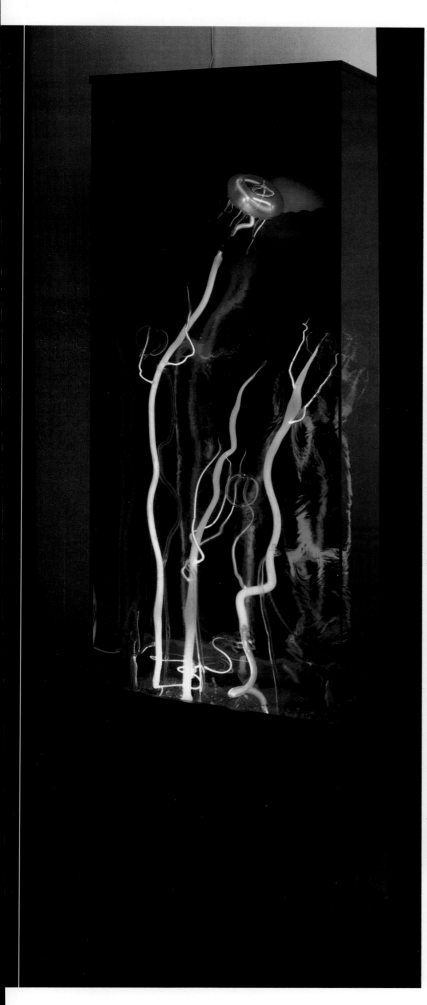

Designer: Peter David
Fabricator: Peter David Studio

This 6'x2'x1' piece, entitled ''Beneath the Sea of Moons,'' consists of neon and blown glass in a case of black glass and wood. A polycarbonate film curtain hangs behind the neon.

Designer: Chic Illuminated Awnings
Fabricator: Chic
Montreal, Quebec, Canada
Client: Il Cortile

This very high class restaurant and caterer wanted something that would indicate exactly what they do yet having subtle messages of class. This brass triangle sign mounted on a concrete column in front of the restaurant is spray painted on acrylic face.

Designer: Terry Martin, Patchen Brownfeld, Inc.
Fabricator: Gannett Outdoor of Arizona
Phoenix, AZ
Client: American West Airlines

Designer:    Craig A. Kraft
Fabricator:   Kraft Studio
              Kensington, MD

Entitled ''Storm Rider'' (1987 ©), this piece consists of
acrylic (hand- and heat-formed and layered); back-
painting on overmask; glass neon tubing; and Densite
— a cast and modeled gypsum polymer. Its dimensions
are 30''x 28''x 8''.

Designer:    Craig A. Kraft
Fabricator:    Kraft Studio
                Kensington, MD

This piece is entitled ''It's Some Kind of Circus!'' (1987
©). It consists of acrylic that is hand- and heat-formed
and layered; glass neon tubing; and Densite, a gypsom
polymer that is cast and modeled. The piece is bent so
that it mounts in a 90° corner. Its dimensions are
38''x 42''x 42''.

# INDEX OF DESIGNERS

# INDEX OF FABRICATORS

# INDEX OF CLIENTS